Persecuted and Forgotten?

A Report on Christians oppressed for their Faith
2007/2008

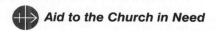

Aid to the Church in Need

Persecuted and Forgotten?
A report on Christians oppressed for their Faith 2007/2008

Edited by John Pontifex and John Newton
With selected extracts from *Report on Religious Freedom in the World*
(ACN 2008)

Published by
Aid to the Church in Need
12–14 Benhill Avenue
Sutton, Surrey
SM1 4DA
United Kingdom
Tel: 020 8642 8668   Email: acn@acnuk.org
Fax: 020 8661 6293   Website: www.acnuk.org
Registered with the Charity Commission No. 1097984

This publication has been part-sponsored by a trustee and benefactor of Aid to the Church in Need.

Cover: Chinese 'Underground' Catholic Bishop John Han Dingxian of Yongnian (Hebei province) in police custody. Still from footage filmed in secret in 2005. Bishop Han died in September 2007 after two years in isolation and a total of 35 years in prison.
Cover design by: Chimera Design Ltd

Printed in the UK by CPI William Clowes, Beccles, NR34 7TL

ISBN 978-0-9553339-5-8

Foreword by Archbishop Georges Casmoussa of Mosul, Iraq

Nothing, it seems, escapes the media's attention. But rarely if ever do we see anything on a matter that is crucial: the suffering that people endure for their religious faith.

I have witnessed – indeed I have experienced for myself – the humiliation, the anguish and the physical agony people have gone through for their beliefs. Not long after the overthrow of Saddam, I was kidnapped while visiting families in my diocese. During my confinement, my captors kept demanding answers about my faith. It was difficult but I remained calm.

Thank God, the next day I was released. But in the years since, others have not been so lucky. Another bishop from Mosul, Paulos Faraj Rahho, priests and lay people have paid the ultimate price. People of all faiths have suffered, but especially Christians. This is true in so many countries.

The persecution of Christians in our world today amounts to a human rights disaster. It is a catastrophe that has been ignored by the media, almost as if a news black-out has been enforced. This book, *Persecuted and Forgotten? 2007/2008*, which looks at those countries where Christians suffer for their faith, helps to redress the balance, putting on record the trials and tribulations people face for remaining true to their beliefs.

In the accounts here, you will see something perhaps unexpected – how persecution has helped us to go deeper into our faith, to discover what Christ really meant by 'take up your Cross and follow me'. Through our sacrifices, we know the truth of those words of Tertullian from so long ago: "The blood of the martyrs is the seed of the Church." Indeed, as we say in my country: "The martyrs' blood is the seed of life itself."

+ B. Georges Casmoussa

+ B. Georges Casmoussa, Syrian Catholic Archbishop of Mosul

Contents

Introduction

"If martyrdom does eventually come, I ask for the strength to go through with it."[1] With these words, Bishop Georgio Bertin describes life as a Christian in his corner of east Africa. The problems he confronts in Somalia are deep-rooted: many Christians, he says, are "very afraid to come to Mass"; churches lie empty and abandoned; Christians receive threats, indeed a religious sister was recently killed; and in neighbouring Djibouti, youths pelted his office with stones.[2]

Persecution is not just the stuff of history; it is a modern-day phenomenon – and nor is it only to be found in the Horn of Africa. In many parts of the world, religious groups of all descriptions experience violence and intimidation – but none more so, it seems, than Christians. Indeed, research strongly indicates that taken as a whole more Christians are oppressed than any other faith community. Leading experts in the field agree that today 200 million Christians suffer for their faith, many of them facing murder and other forms of violence.[3] It is a figure quoted by a number of sources.[4] Some go on to add a further 350 million Christians who experience lesser forms of oppression: discrimination and restrictions concerning religious practice.[5] Others go on to claim: "Millions of Christians face discrimination and harassment every day as a result of their faith."[6]

Compiled and produced by *Aid to the Church in Need* (ACN), the Catholic charity for persecuted and other suffering Christians, this report delves behind the statistics to show the human cost of the suffering. The book shows how individual families and local communities live in the shadow of violence and discrimination – affecting their jobs, their pay, their children's schools, their health and sometimes their lives too.

The principal source for *Persecuted and Forgotten? 2007/2008* is the 2008 ACN publication *Report on Religious Freedom in the World*, a comprehensive global survey, drawing on research and analysis by leading experts. Concentrating on selected extracts tackling oppression of Christians, *Persecuted and Forgotten? 2007/2008* corroborates the results of this intensive investigation with independent findings – first-hand ACN accounts, exclusive interviews and on-the-spot reportage. This material is supplemented by reports from major human rights institutions and Christian organisations. As a follow-up to the 2006 *Persecuted and*

5

Forgotten? publication, this edition examines more countries and does so in greater depth.

The subject under investigation needs to be clearly established. Over-use has emptied the term 'persecution' of meaning and so the book adheres to the *Oxford English Dictionary* definition which describes persecution as a malicious act motivated by religious hostility.

The book is of course mainly concerned with countries where Christians are persecuted the most. However, it also assesses other parts of the world – including some popular holiday destinations – where few would imagine the scale of religious rights' abuses.

Running through the book are two prevailing themes which go in opposite directions. The first concerns certain communist and other traditionally atheistic regimes; after decades of intolerance, these countries are now showing an openness towards Christianity or at least a grudging acceptance of its place in society. The second and more dominant theme is the rising tide of extremism in a number of Islamic countries; in many such regimes, the persecution towards non-Muslims and especially Christians is so severe that the Church's very survival is now under threat.

Looking at many of the communist and other left-leaning countries as a whole, it is clear that over a number of years seismic changes have taken place which have contributed to a significant re-evaluation of the role of religion in society. In regimes traditionally hostile towards Christianity, it has emerged that attitudes are softening. Principal causes for this include a decline in Marxist atheistic ideology and a weary acceptance of the durability of religious belief.

For example in February 2008, Vatican Secretary of State Cardinal Tarcisio Bertone visited Cuba and opened the first completely new church building sanctioned by the government in modern times. It came at about the time President Fidel Castro ceded power to his brother, Raúl. Elsewhere, in Vietnam, a summer 2008 ACN project assessment trip revealed a Church enjoying improved confidence and status after laws were passed reducing controls on religious activities. Such developments have been keenly noted by both the Vatican and the US State Department. In former Soviet countries, Pope Benedict XVI's reputation as a world-class theologian has helped win improved recognition for Catholics. Signs of hope are also visible in China where the Church's massive growth and increased religiosity among Communist Party officials have caused the regime to show greater restraint. Church leaders in China now say that across the country 200,000 adults convert to Catholicism every year. Meanwhile, some reports claim that there are as many as 80 million Christians in China,[7] double the figure most often quoted. That said, China's spring 2008 clampdown on uprisings in Tibet shows how such progress can easily go into reverse, a situation that applies to many other similar countries.

In marked contrast are some of the major Islamic states. The 2006 *Persecuted and Forgotten* reported on a post 9/11 Islamist backlash against Christians, many of whom have faced the largely bogus charge of being pro-US In many Muslim countries, Christians have felt they are paying the price for "the greed and iniquities of the Western nations", as Archbishop Lawrence Saldanha of Lahore put it in a statement to ACN.[8] In the last two years, anti-Christian radicalism has dramatically worsened amid a rising tide of fundamentalism. The intolerance has fed off increasing anti-West sentiment and the fall-out from the so-called 'War on Terror'. Now, in key regions, Christians are told: abandon your faith or face the consequences. For some, failure to comply means eviction from their homes, violence and even murder. An age-old atmosphere of co-existence and even friendly relations has suddenly soured. For many Christians the pressure has proved too great. Many no longer feel welcome in an Islamic society reducing them to *dhimmi* status (i.e. a non-Muslim subject of a state governed by *Shari'a* law). Stripped of basic human rights, they receive little or no protection in court. Furthermore, they face extra taxation, suffer discrimination in the workplace, are pressurised to convert to Islam, and are forced to comply with a strict dress code, including the veil. But by far the most significant problem is the threat of a charge of proselytism. Far from being a question of haranguing people in the street with Christian literature or 'Bible bashing' on the radio, in some Muslim countries the threat involves the mere presence of a church or a cross or even a passing comment to a stranger. It is an offence punishable by imprisonment, the lash or worse. Meanwhile, Muslims who convert – men especially – are threatened with the death penalty and almost certainly must go into hiding and seek asylum abroad.

In response to such intense intimidation, the emigration of Christians from some Muslim countries has now become a mass exodus. *Persecuted and*

7

Forgotten? 2007/2008 charts the miserable course of Christianity in Iraq. In 1987, an official census recorded a total of 1.4 million faithful; by mid-2008, there were less than 400,000. A high proportion of these are displaced Christians, who have fled their homes in the last four years and are now seeking a new life abroad, preferably in the West. The full extent of the crisis only became known in the West in March 2008 after the kidnapping of Chaldean Archbishop Paulos Faraj Rahho of Mosul, north-west Iraq. Two weeks later his body was found dumped in a shallow grave. Speaking to ACN on his way to the funeral outside Mosul, Chaldean Archbishop Louis Sako described Archbishop Rahho as "a man who gave his life for his Church and his people". Archbishop Sako graphically described the people's sense of loss and fear, saying: "Things have been getting worse and worse." And in a touching reference to the Church's preparations for Easter, he continued: "Holy Week for us has come early and today is our Good Friday; we are living out Christ's passion spiritually and at all levels. The Christians were clinging on to the hope that the archbishop would one day be able to come back and support them."[9]

Archbishop Rahho's death demonstrated just how far the situation has unraveled for the Church in the region. Christian migration is a problem that affects the whole Middle East. In a situation of flux, few statistics are reliable but the best estimates available give a sense of the scale of the crisis. In the Holy Land, the Christian population has slumped from 20 percent to less than 1.5 percent in 60 years. In Lebanon, the Christian community has dwindled by more than 30 percent within the last 25 years. And in Iran, the Christian population has plummeted by two-thirds since the 1970s. Christians in the region feel abandoned to their fate by a culture in the West marked by ignorance and ambivalence.

Pope Benedict XVI, however, is under no illusion about the reality of the suffering Church. In early 2008, he said: "This 21st century has also opened under the banner of martyrdom."[10]

Again and again, *Aid to the Church in Need* is asked who, if anyone, will come to their aid to ensure that in this region, the Cradle of Christianity, the community of faith will still be standing a generation from now. The Pope has called on ACN to make the Church in the Middle East a priority for aid. In September 2007, leading ACN figures marked the charity's 60th anniversary by gathering at the Pope's summer residence outside Rome.

There, they were told: "Churches in the Middle East are today threatened in their very existence."[11] In addition to religious leaders, politicians and diplomats on all sides frequently acknowledge the key role of Christians in nation-building, a process they believe to be impossible without them.

Looking beyond the Middle East, *Persecuted and Forgotten? 2007/2008* identifies other countries affected by the rise of Islamic radicalism. Among them is Algeria where by summer 2008, half of Algeria's 52 Protestant churches were reportedly closed – all within six months.[12] Elsewhere, when Pakistan's Catholic bishops met Benedict XVI at their five-yearly 'Ad Limina' meeting in June 2008, they told the Pope that attitudes towards the Church had changed beyond recognition. Archbishop Saldanha, president of Pakistan's Catholic Bishops' Conference, reportedly said to the Pontiff that in the past the Church was respected for its work in education and medicine. "But today", he continued, "we carry out our mission in a hostile and conservative Islamic milieu that is increasingly extremist, intolerant and militant."[13]

The long-term outcome of such renewed pressure on Christians is unclear but what is beyond doubt is that across the Islamic world, the Church is threatened as never before. The Pope hails "the shining witness of those... heroic to the point of martyrdom". It is *Aid to the Church in Need*'s task to hold up this "shining" example for all the world to see.

But even in the worst situations, hope remains. *Persecuted and Forgotten? 2007/2008* shows how the work of many Church leaders has opened up opportunities for Cooperation, renewed trust and mutual respect. Here, and elsewhere, the work of *Aid to the Church in Need* is crucial. With more than 5,000 projects in nearly 140 countries, the charity is bringing Christ to the world – helping to train seminarians and religious Sisters, build churches, support poor priests, teach youngsters, provide *Child's Bibles* and send emergency aid to refugees. At ACN's 60th anniversary celebrations, Pope Benedict XVI urged the charity to remain faithful to the legacy of its founder, Fr Werenfried van Straaten, adding: "Be assured of the gratitude and prayers of the Successor of Peter for your work, which is an eloquent testimony to the love of God. Please continue to let people know that God is there for us as a loving father."[14] In a broken, grieving world torn apart by pain and division, reaching out to the poor and the persecuted is a task that should never be forgotten.

Algeria

Population	Religions	Christian Population
33.5 million[15]	Sunni Muslim 79% Shi'a Muslim 18% Christian 2.5% Other 0.5%	80,000

In the first half of 2008, nearly 30 churches were forcibly closed and dozens of Christians were arrested on charges of 'proselytism'. Reporting on these developments, human rights organisations blamed the clampdown on Christianity on the new religion law brought into effect in late 2006 and enforced by two presidential decrees of May 2007.[16]

Under the regulations, non-Muslims found guilty of evangelising among Muslims – either directly or indirectly through welfare work including schools and hospitals – are liable to a prison sentence of up to five years or a fine rising to US$14,000. The law requires all non-Islamic 'religious meetings' to be held in authorised premises and failure to comply could lead to three years in prison and a fine of up to US$4,200.

The distribution of religious literature and other publicity material is strictly controlled, as are donations. A government-appointed commission is now responsible for deciding on non-Muslim religious buildings deemed suitable for worship. Religious freedom campaigners say the law's vague language will be exploited by anti-Christian extremists. Charities and human rights organisations have warned that Christians are directly threatened by the document's condemnation of initiatives which could 'shake the faith of a Muslim'.

Despite its opening remarks defending religious freedom, key articles of the 2006 law are seen as clashing with Algeria's constitution. Article 36 of the 1996 constitution declares that religious freedom is inviolable. The new law is aimed at Evangelical preachers but Catholic churches are often targeted because the local media ignores denominational differences.

Often seen as outsiders, most Christians in Algeria are foreigners (Europeans, Lebanese, students from sub-Saharan Africa and some Americans). Amid a rise in fundamentalist Islam, in early 2008 the Algerian press was accused of stoking intolerance by highlighting stories of Muslims converting to Christianity.

May 2007: The local authorities of 48 *wilayas* (departments) invited all the Catholics present to leave Algeria, following a directive from central government. Those responsible for the Catholic Church appealed to the highest Algerian authorities to get the decision annulled.[17] Soon after, the *Centre social du Corso*, a Church-run social centre in the capital, Algiers, was closed down.[18]

June 2007: Five young Christians were brought to trial in the city of Tizi-Ouzou accused of proselytism. One of them was trapped by a plain-clothes policeman, who asked for Christian publications and then arrested him after being given a Bible.[19]

November 2007: Without being offered any explanation, four Brazilian Catholic voluntary workers were ordered to leave the country within two weeks, even though their papers were in order. This provision was annulled later thanks to the Brazilian Ambassador.[20]

February 2008: The Algerian authorities rejected half of the visas requested by the Catholic Church for replacing personnel.[21]

February 2008: About 30 sub-Saharan students attending a weekend course of Biblical studies in Tizi-Ouzou were ordered to leave Algeria. The decision was revoked following an intervention by the Senegalese Ambassador.[22]

March 2008: Police told Pastor Salah Chalah to close his 1,200-member Full Gospel Church, in Tizi-Ousou. Police also issued notice to a second pastor, Mustapha Krireche, to close down his church in Tizi-Ousou's Nouvelle Ville district. In the four months after October 2007, 19 congregations received written orders to shut down. Additionally, two independent congregations were told to close their doors, according to Mustapha Krim, President of Protestant Church of Algeria.[23]

March 2008: A woman named Habiba Qawider was accused of "practising a non-Muslim religion without authorisation" after she was found carrying Christian literature on a public bus. Qawider was ordered off a bus while travelling outside her home town Tiaret. She was handcuffed after police found some 10 Bibles and books on Christianity in her handbag. The public prosecutor asked for a three-year prison term for Habiba. In June 2008 the retiring Archbishop of Algiers asked the authorities to drop all charges,

11

following the suspension of her trial. The results of his intervention are not yet known.[24]

April 2008: A Christian was handed a two-year suspended sentence for "proselytism". The individual plans to appeal the two-year suspended sentence and a fine of 100,000 dinar (US$1,540).[25]

May 2008: Rachid, Djallil, Sami, Abdelkader, Mohamed and Chabane – all of them Christians – were accused of distributing religious material to convert Muslims and practising non-Muslim worship without authorization. They were arrested despite not being found in possession of religious literature or other Christian items. The public prosecutor asked the court in the town of Tiaret to sentence each of the Christians to two years in prison and fine them 500,000 Algerian dinars (US$8,000). The prosecutor alleged that the six Christians were gathered to worship at the house of Rachid, who is one of the defendants.[26]

May 2008: Reports came in showing that half of Algeria's 52 Protestant churches had been closed within the previous six months. The reports, originating from *Open Doors USA*, said that the churches had been shut down following either an official written order or a verbal warning. Some of the churches had congregations of more than 1,000. Persecution watchdogs warned that all the Protestant churches would be forced to close before the end of 2008. *Open Doors* staff linked the closures to the religion laws passed in 2006.[27]

Profile: Bishop Alphonse Georger from Algeria[28]

His predecessor was assassinated. He requires security during parish visits. His faithful can only pray in places registered for the purpose. And yet in an interview of more than an hour there is no trace of bitterness or resentment in his manner.

By any standards, Bishop Alphonse Georger has an unenviable task. Born in Lorraine, he was, in his own words "ordained priest for Algeria". More than 40 years later, he is acutely aware of how much Christians have suffered. The Church that was once a state-recognised religion is now subject to institutionalised discrimination. Christians are even prevented from praying in their own homes.

It was not always thus. Bishop Georger's first experience of Algeria was between 1960 and 1962 when he did military service in what was then an outpost of the French colonial empire. By the time he returned as a priest, the north African country had won independence, sparking an exodus of Christians. But, as late as 1976, there were still many French, Italian and Chinese people who took work in the oil-rich country. A full 14 years on from independence, the Church still continued with public works such as schools and indeed the future Bishop Georger was headmaster of one such school. All that was to end when the schools were nationalised. In the years since, it has become steadily more difficult for Christians and now their work is confined largely to libraries and a certain amount of social work.

According to official statistics, before 1960 there were 355,000 Catholics in Bishop Georger's diocese of Oran, Algeria – this amounted to nearly 18 percent of the total population.[29] Today there are barely 400 Catholics in a population which in 50 years has risen from 1.9 million to 7.25 million.

The pressure on the Christian community mounted to the point where 19 priests and religious were murdered within a two-year period. Among the dead were Bishop Georger's predecessor, Bishop Pierre Claverie OP.

It came at the height of a campaign to stamp out activities thought to encourage apostasy from Islam. Until his tragic death in August 1996, Bishop Claverie worked on social cohesion projects aimed at bringing together people of different backgrounds. Bishop Georger reflected: "The problem was that some of the Muslims attending thought the Church was trying to convert people – which definitely wasn't the case."

If it seemed that replacing Bishop Claverie was like being handed a poisoned chalice, Bishop Georger is good at hiding his feelings. In a diocese the size of Bavaria, the bishop now has 17 priests and nearly 50 Sisters working with him. It is a far cry from the days when part of modern-day Algeria was home to St Augustine of Hippo. At about the time he was bishop, in the fifth century, there were more than 200 dioceses across this region of Africa.

The 2006 religion laws mean a bad situation has just got worse. Non-Muslims in Algeria face tight restrictions about where "religious meetings" can be held and 'inciting' people to convert is banned. The laws carry maximum penalties of a US$14,000 fine and five years in prison.[30]

Bishop Georger is well aware that times ahead will be tough. Already, life is hard. When asked about future priests, he replied brusquely: "No, we don't have a seminary – it had to be closed." But Bishop Georger, now 72, is determined to look on the bright side of life. He describes an old people's home run by some sisters who receive almsgiving from pious Muslims. "Each Friday is a day of prayer and people come with bread and recently on the feast of Abraham, they received 50 lambs. All this means the Sisters can keep the old people's home in very good shape. It's a kind of miracle."

There is hope elsewhere too. Outside Oran is a pilgrimage site on a hilltop. Bishop Georger described visiting it after being made a bishop. It had been left untended for 10 years and the shrine itself was used to house sheep. But now a church is being built – thanks to *Aid to the Church in Need*. He finishes with a flourish: "You see: we are living without fear. Jesus said: 'Do not be afraid'. I think it is you, the Church in the West, who are afraid. We must not be afraid. Most of the people we live with are friends. They are what we should be: a sign of hope."

Bangladesh

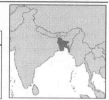

Population	Religions	Christian Population
158 million	Muslim 84% Hindu 14% Buddhist 1% Christian 1%	1.5 million

A dramatic rise in extremist activity in 2007-08 has alarmed Christian and other minority groups. Reports show that Christians increasingly feel they are offered little or no protection, despite a constitution which describes religious freedom as a priority. The caretaker government, in place after a state of emergency was declared on 11th January 2007, has been accused of increasingly bowing to extremist groups in a bid to shore-up its power-base. The new administration was further weakened by a series of crises, such as the November 2007 cyclone, which stretched resources almost to breaking point.

By then, the government had finally given official recognition to *madrassas* (Islamic schools), a significant proportion of which are considered to be deeply intolerant of other religions. According to some sources, within 20 years the number of *madrassas* has grown from barely 4,000 to 64,000. In tribal areas especially, Christians and other minority groups experience discrimination. Extremist groups put pressure on them to convert, sometimes threatening violence. This persecution against religious minorities, which includes the Ahmadis,[31] often has the aim of depriving families and entire villages of their properties. Minority religious groups can only hope that the long-awaited general elections, postponed in January 2007, will give the government renewed impetus to crack down on militant activity.

March 2007: Catholic Bishop Bejoy Nicephorus D'Cruze of Khulna, in the south-west of the country, reported to ACN that the faithful in his diocese needed protection from Islamic extremists. He said: "In Bangladesh the Christians are a small minority; we are afraid of extremism." Christians have often been charged with trying to secure 'forced conversions' – persuading the poor to convert in return for economic rewards. Ill-founded rumours of this kind have sometimes triggered well-orchestrated violence, carried out by Muslims and sometimes Buddhists.[32]

June 2007: A group of Muslims attacked some recent converts to Christianity, giving them 24 hours to leave the country or be beaten. The violence that followed left a number of people wounded and one house destroyed. The attacks followed the baptism two weeks earlier of 42 people who had converted from Islam. The media and local authorities justified the threats, blaming them on "the Christian practice" of "forced conversions". Local religious experts, however, said the conversions were not carried out by force or through deception.

August 2007: Sources in the Nilphamari district reported that local Muslims and international Islamist missionaries were hauling recently converted Christians to mosques and demanding that they abandon their new faith. Local Christian leaders said 27 Christians were forced to revert to Islam. Police intervened, providing protection to those Christians thought to be at risk. However, after a week the security forces left and Muslim extremists began dragging male converts to a mosque and forcing them to sign blank papers or declarations of a return to Islam. Abdul Hossen said that he was told that if he did not comply he would be hung upside down from a tree and lacerated with a knife. Mr Hossen said that he was offered US$75 and a mobile phone if he abandoned Christianity.[33]

August 2007: A Bangladesh court in a district of the capital, Dhaka, handed out death sentences to an extremist found guilty of killing converts to Christianity. Mohammad Salauddin, a leading figure in the banned Islamic militant group *Jamayetul Mujahideen Bangladesh* (JMB), confessed to slitting the throat of a man named Roy on 23rd April 2003. In his written statement, Salauddin said he killed Roy "because he was engaged in converting Muslims into Christians by showing films on Jesus".[34]

January 2008: Rahima Beoa, a 70-year-old woman in Rangpur district, sustained severe burns in an attack, apparently linked to claims that she was about to convert to Christianity. Khaled Mintu, regional district supervisor of the Isha-E-Jamat Bangladesh church, said: "The unknown attackers wanted to burn the elderly woman alive because they came to know that she would be a Christian in the next month." Mrs Beoa is mother-in-law of Ashraful Islam who, along with his wife, became a Christian two years ago. Close relatives and neighbours were said to be angry with the couple for their conversion from Islam.[35]

Belarus

Population	Religions	Christian Population
10 million	Christian 70% Non religious 24% Atheist 5% Other 1%	7 million

A 2002 law on religious freedom made Russian Orthodoxy the country's official religion. But it also recognised both the "spiritual, cultural and historical role of the Catholic Church" and the "inalienability of the Lutheran Church from the country's history". The law's opponents criticised its ban on prayer meetings in private homes and its complex registration procedures concerning other religious services. People petitioning against the law collected the 50,000 signatures required for the matter to be referred to the Constitutional Court. Orthodox, Catholics and Protestants all helped collect signatures. However, government bodies rejected the petition in late March 2008, claiming that reports of religious freedom violations "do not correspond with reality".[36]

Protestant communities without their own property encounter obstacles when wanting to meet for worship. Registered religious organisations may rent secular premises, but only with the approval of the relevant local state authority. Landlords frequently renege on contracts with Protestant groups soon after the authorities are informed. For the Protestants, such problems can be alleviated by ecumenical Cooperation. Although banned from renting premises in Grodno, the charismatic Living Word Church meets in the local Catholic church.[37] Rebuilding can also be a problem: a Baptist congregation in the same region was refused permission to rebuild its 1920's wooden church in brick; no reason was given.[38]

Even though Belarusian authorities exercise tight controls over religious activities, President Alexander Lukashenko is generally open to the larger religious communities, and on 19th September 2007 the first of a series of round-table talks was held between Deputy Prime Minister Aleksandr Kosinets and the leaders of all the religions recognised in Minsk, the capital city.

The largely foreign-born (particularly Polish) Catholic clergy face considerable red tape over entry visas. In the Catholic Church 190 out of 281 priests are foreign-born. A quota system limits the number of foreign

17

clerics allowed in the country; by the same token, any religious minister who moves to another parish within Belarus must get a new visa. A growing number of clergy (Protestant as well as Catholic) and religious have been refused entry. The chairman of the Catholic Bishops' Conference of Belarus, Bishop Aleksandr Kaszkiewicz of Grodno, wrote a letter of protest and called on the faithful to take part in a week of prayer in the cathedral to declare their opposition.[39] Deputy Prime Minister Kosinets said: "We are in favour of clergymen who have Belarusian nationality [...because] it is not possible to conduct religious activities without speaking Belarusian or Russian, or understanding how people think, or knowing their customs and traditions."

March 2007: In Gomel, Belarus' second largest city, in the south west of the country, Belarusian KGB agents raided an Orthodox prayer meeting held in a flat. The prayers were attended by 15 Orthodox believers loyal to the Moscow Patriarchate. The group were told they were targeted "because we were conducting unsanctioned religious activity. They said we were a pseudo-Christian sect engaged in the recruitment of members."[40]

May 2007: State officials raided the Pentecost service of the John the Baptist Pentecostal Church in the capital city, Minsk. Pastor Antoni Bokun was arrested and held overnight at a police station. He was fined 20 times the minimum monthly wage for holding an "unsanctioned mass meeting".[41]

June 2007: Evangelical pastor Jaroslaw Lukasik was deported after police annulled his residence permit for "activities aimed at harming the national security of the Republic of Belarus in the sphere of inter-confessional relations." He had been living in the country since 1999 with his Belarusian wife and three children, all of whom remain in Belarus.[42]

June 2007: Pastor Antoni Bokun was handed a three-day prison term for leading a communion service, making him the third person to be imprisoned in post-Soviet Belarus for "religious activity".[43]

July 2007: Oleg Bobrik, a regional Ideology Department official, attempted to break up a holiday camp for members of a charismatic church in Minsk. The local district executive committee had given written permission for the family holiday camp, but Bobrik claimed that the camp did not conform to either the Religion Law or Education Ministry instructions regulating health camps.[44]

October 2007: Pastor Dmitri Podlobko was given an official warning to stop "illegal" religious activity. It followed efforts by local state officials to stop the Living Word Church from holding a Sunday service on private premises.[45]

December 2007: Polish Catholic priest Grzegorz Chudek of Trinity Parish Church, in the town of Rechytsa, was ordered to leave the country. More than 700 of the local congregation appealed to President Lukashenko on the priest's behalf. He was ordered to leave by 1st December but his visa was subsequently extended by two months. However, during this period he was banned from working in the parish.[46]

February 2008: A pastor was threatened with a fine after members of the New Life Church in Minsk stopped state inspectors from entering the property. The officials had powers to impose fines. It came after a court indefinitely adjourned proceedings to decide the fate of the church building.[47]

March 2008: Pavel Nozdrya, who helped organise a petition to amend the 2002 Religion Law, lost his job as an electrician at a local university. He was one of seven members of a charismatic youth group, who were meeting in a private house on 29th February when it was raided by local Ideology Department officials. A police officer, who visited the same house on Sunday, 9th March, said he was responding to a report that human sacrifice would be taking place there.[48]

Bosnia–Herzegovina

Population	Religions	Christian Population
4 million	Christian 46% Muslim 40% Other 14%	1.8 million

Even though religious freedom is enshrined in the 1995 constitution (Article 2), there are alarming cases of discrimination and violence. Muslims, Catholics and Orthodox Serbs have all reported many cases of aggression and religious intolerance. Religious practice is relatively low but there are some areas where religion is taken very seriously. Examples of this include the Croatian Catholic communities in Bosnia, where they are a minority. They find themselves in a difficult position, fighting for survival in an environment which is becoming increasingly Islamic.

During 2007, attacks on religious buildings, symbols, and ministers rose. The Catholic Church, the Serbian Orthodox Church, the Protestant and the Muslim communities were all victim to aggression and vandalism. The judiciary continue to be unhelpful, and police rarely arrest those responsible for vandalism against religious buildings or for attacks on ministers.

Current legislation states that, with the support of at least 300 faithful, Christian leaders can apply to build a new church by writing to the Ministry of Justice. A decision is required within 30 days and appeals against the ruling can be made to the Council of Ministers.

Parents have the right to enrol their children in private schools for religious reasons. Many towns and cities have faith-based schools – Muslim, Catholic and Serbian Orthodox. Church-funded Catholic schools, under diocesan control, work towards religious and social reconciliation.

For some time, the four largest religious communities have requested the return of buildings confiscated by the communist regime. Failing that, they have asked for compensation. The State Commission for Restitution is drafting a national law on this issue. Until then such issues are decided at a local level.

To tackle areas of conflict or disagreement, the leaders of the main religions continue to meet at the Interreligious Council of Bosnia and Herzegovina.

The Catholic and Orthodox churches meet regularly to discuss common issues and ideas, which many hope will lead towards greater cooperation. During a week of ecumenical dialogue in April 2007, Bosnia and Herzegovina's Cardinal Vinko Puljic, Archbishop of Vrhbosna, presided at a religious service in the Orthodox cathedral of Sarajevo. Elsewhere in the city, Metropolitan Nikolai, Bishop of Dabar Bosna and leader of the Serbian Orthodox Church of Bosnia and Herzegovina, held a service in the Catholic cathedral.

April 2007: After six years' work, the Holy See and the Bosnian government signed a draft Concordat governing the legal status of the Catholic Church in Bosnia. The agreement acknowledges the respective independence of the two parties, but also their willingness to cooperate. It also established the legal framework for relations between the state and the Holy See.[49]

Burma (Myanmar)

Population	Religions	Christian Pop.
49 million	Buddhist 80% Animist 7%, Christian 6% Muslim 3.5% Other 3.5%	3 million

The situation concerning human rights and religious freedom is deteriorating in Burma. In August and September 2007, Buddhist monks led the so-called "Saffron Revolution", a demonstration against the abuses and repressive policies of the military regime which has held power since 1962. Following the monks' lead, thousands took to the streets, but by the end of September the military junta had unleashed its forces against the protesters, especially targeting Buddhist monks and monasteries. Official figures put the death toll at 10, but the real number will probably never be known. NGOs have said that across the country hundreds died and thousands were arrested.

The Catholic Church urged clergy not to demonstrate. Archbishop Charles Maung Bo of Yangon (Rangoon), the former capital, told *AsiaNews* that instead of protesting, people should pray "because we are a minority and to carry on with our work we must be cautious." Benedict XVI assured the country of his "intense and concerned prayer". He urged the Church to do the same so "that a peaceful solution [to the crisis] can be found for the good of the country."[50]

Many of Burma's Christians are persecuted because they belong to certain ethnic minorities such as the Karen, who have been fighting the central government for recognition and the right to self-determination. The Karen people have been subjected to the most appalling atrocities and, according to Lord Howell of Guildford, were rounded up, shot at and slaughtered "in a manner reminiscent of the Nazi era".[51]

The military regime restricts evangelisation work as well as initiatives to import and distribute Christian books. All publications are subject to controls and censorship. Limited consignments of religious literature in minority languages have occasionally been allowed without prior approval by the censorship board. However it is still illegal to import Bibles written in local languages.

"Even though we can pray, celebrate Mass and recite the Rosary, there is no true religious freedom," said a group of Yangon (Rangoon) Catholics. They went on to state that priests were not allowed to discuss or pray for peace, justice or improved human rights. The group added that people were living in fear of arrest or torture. "We are all subject to the law," they said, "but the junta is above it and uses every method to silence the population".

The military regime has caused major problems for the Church. Difficulties setting up new parishes mean that in some places a single priest is in charge of vast areas. In some regions, a parish priest is only able to meet his parishioners and say Mass for them three times a year.

According to Christians in Chin state, since 1997 the government has stopped any churches being built. This claim emerges in the US State Department's annual Report on Religious Freedom. But other reports indicate that the Catholic Church has not faced the same problems as Protestants. In cities including Yangon (Rangoon) and Mandalay the authorities have allowed some Christian communities to build new centres, but only if they agreed not to put religious symbols on public view. Despite such restrictions, the Burmese Church is growing. There are many vocations and conversions among the animist minorities, and a number of priests and nuns go abroad on mission.

December 2007: Following the uprising in the autumn and the subsequent clampdown, the bishops asked their faithful to cancel the usual Christmas celebrations. Catholics from a dozen or more villages in Chin State in western Burma have traditionally met for a large festive gathering, climaxing in a Christmas service, but the local bishop sent an urgent message urging that the traditional festivities be cancelled and requesting that the faithful hold low-key celebrations within their own separate villages instead. A religious Sister from Burma said no reasons were given for the bishop's actions, but fear of a government clampdown was a probable factor.[52]

China

Population	Religions	Christian Pop.
1.3 billion	Atheist 50%	40 million
	Chinese religions 29%	
	Other 10%,	
	Buddhist 8%, Christian 3%	

China's dream of an Olympics show-casing the country's record-breaking progress was beset by a series of setbacks during the run-up to the Beijing games. The international community's concerns about China's human rights record resurfaced after the regime's decisive intervention following the spring 2008 Tibet uprising. Seemingly undaunted, the Chinese Communist Party pushed on with its ambitious plans for Beijing 2008, a golden opportunity to celebrate the country's growing global profile.

Although officially still atheist, the People's Republic of China has taken unprecedented steps which appear to be aimed at increasing cooperation with religious groups. The topic of religion was formally discussed at a plenary session of the Communist Party's politburo in December 2007. President Hu Jintao, the party's Secretary General, also took part.[53] But other sources[54] said that a primary reason for the high-level discussions was the party's growing concern at the rise of religious practice across China, especially in rural areas. Sources say that communist officials have abandoned Marxist views about the imminent demise of religious practice. As a result, they increasingly seek support from faith groups for community projects.

Research by two Professors, Tong Shijun and Liu Zhongyu, from a university in Shanghai, showed that in 2006/2007 there were at least 300 million followers of religion in China, more than treble the government's estimate released only two years previously.[55] According to these reports, this phenomenal growth increased the Communist Party's fears of civil disobedience. Such concerns were exacerbated by the 2007 uprisings in Burma, a close collaborator with China. Another factor explaining government nervousness were reports that religious groups planned to hijack the Olympics to highlight reports of oppression by the regime.

The Church, however, is particularly problematic for the regime. Reports indicate party concern at statistics showing that Christianity is now the fastest growing religion in China. Christians may number 40 million,[56] far higher than Beijing's estimate of 23 million (18 million Protestants and five million Catholics).

Religious leaders say Christianity's growth stems from a new thirst for freedom and knowledge following generations of Marxist oppression. Whatever the reasons, Christianity in all its forms is viewed with suspicion – and in some cases outright contempt – by the officials.

For the Catholic Church, the 2007-08 period was dominated by Pope Benedict XVI's pastoral letter of 27th May 2007. In it, the Pontiff appealed for greater unity between the so-called 'Underground' Catholic Church (not recognised by the government) and the (state-approved) 'Official' Catholic Church. The letter very respectfully asked the political authorities to guarantee the Church freedom of religious practice. A serious obstacle to improved Sino-Vatican relations is the appointment of bishops, a major dispute dating back generations. Indeed the year before the Pope's letter, the Chinese Catholic Patriotic Association (CCPA), an arm of government which seeks control of the Church, had insisted on the ordination of three bishops without prior authorisation by the Holy See.

Most government-sponsored episcopal ordinations are eventually approved by the Holy See. The ordination of bishops for dioceses in various parts of the country that took place in the autumn of 2007 received papal backing. But delays in obtaining Vatican assent point towards behind-the-scenes tensions still dogging the Church's relations with China. Recent statistics show that more than 90 percent of bishops in China – both 'Official' and 'Underground' – are approved by the Holy See. At the time of writing, at least 12 Catholic bishops and a similar number of priests are either behind bars or in some way prevented from carrying out their ministry.[57] But while disputes over bishops frequently receive international media coverage, the ongoing – and in some cases worsening – attacks on Christians continue largely unnoticed by the rest of the world.

January 2007: Officials of the Public Security Bureau, regarded as secret police, raided a Protestant church gathering in Baoding city (Hebei province). The meeting was unusual because it was held in a local Communist Party school and was hosted by the school's vice president, presumably a member of the Chinese Communist Party. The incident is seen as symptomatic of increased religious affiliation among Party membership. One-third of the Party's 60-70 million members are reported to be religious adherents.[58]

April 2007: A Christian woman, seven months pregnant, was dragged kicking and screaming from her home to a hospital by 10 officials from the Family Planning Commission in Baise city (Guangxi Province) south-west China. She and her husband, Pastor Yage 'James', wanted to keep the baby because of their Christian principles. At the hospital, she received an injection to induce the birth. Sources say 40 other pregnant women were forcibly moved to the Youjiang District People's Hospital in Baise city to have abortions.[59]

Summer 2007: Two priests from Wenzhou, Father Shao Zhumin and Father Jiang Sunian, were released and had to receive medical treatment for heart, respiratory and hearing problems due to harsh prison conditions.

August 2007: Liu Bainian, General Secretary of the Chinese Catholic Patriotic Association (CCPA), the government arm responsible for regulating the Church, criticised the Pope's letter to China (27th May 2007) at a celebration of the CCPA's 50th anniversary. According to Western diplomats, he branded the document a new "imperialistic" and "colonizing" initiative and compared it to the actions of 19th century empire-building European powers.

He called the letter a "bad document" and said it was "badly translated into Chinese". He spoke out against distributing the letter and called for a block on public access to all websites hosting the letter such as those of the Vatican and local Catholic churches. In the district of Qingxiu, near the city of Nanning (Guangxi province, south-west China), the police confiscated and destroyed copies of a parish bulletin, which contained extracts of the Papal letter. The Nanning branch of the Government-run Department for Religious Affairs launched a campaign against the Vatican's "penetration" into the life of the Church. It demanded that priests and other religious leaders take part in "re-education" programmes (sometimes dubbed 'brain-washing') to make them "acknowledge" their mistake.[60]

September 2007: Bishop John Han Dingxian of Yongnian (Hebei province) died after two years in isolation and a total of 35 years in prison. Hours before his death in hospital, his relatives were summoned to see him. But none of his clergy or faithful were allowed to visit him or give him the

Sacrament of the Sick. Within a few hours of his death (on 9th September), his body was removed from the hospital under cover of darkness and then cremated. His remains were deposited in a marked grave in a public cemetery. Relatives, clergy and faithful were not permitted to be present during the proceedings. Catholics in the diocese speculated that the police wished to hide "evidence" of possible torture. ACN has learned from well-placed sources that the government continued to restrict visits to the grave. One man, who cannot be named without putting him at risk, said: "We are so tired of these difficulties," but later added: "but the sufferings of this time are as nothing compared to the glory of God."[61]

October 2007: Church leader and human rights activist Hua Huiqi was admitted to hospital unconscious after being attacked. He was under close surveillance after being released from prison in July 2007 where he served a six-month sentence for "obstructing justice". Hua Huiqi offers assistance to people wishing to present petitions to the government. He has challenged alleged confiscation of homes in Beijing.[62]

November 2007: 'Underground' Catholic priest Father Wang Zhong, from Xiwanzi diocese (Hebei) 150 miles north of Beijing, was sentenced to three years in prison for organising celebrations for the consecration of a church in Guyan. A report of the trial stressed that permits for the building's construction had been issued by the Department for Religious Affairs. Father Zhong had been arrested on 24th July 2007 and was placed in total isolation and forbidden from receiving visitors. He was not allowed to organise legal representation at his trial or prepare his defence. Father Zhong's imprisonment is being seen as the latest government initiative to intimidate priests and faithful in his diocese. The co-adjutor bishop, Yao Liang, who leads a diocese of 15,000, was at the time of writing reported as still missing following his arrest on 30th July 2006. Two of his priests and two lay-faithful are in prison.[63]

November 2007: Father Zeng Zhongliang, rector of the seminary of Yuijang diocese (Jiangxi province, central China), was arrested with one of his seminarians, Wang Bin, while they were visiting Guangdong province (southern China). They were imprisoned in Yuijang. They were arrested a few days after a meeting with all priests of the diocese, organised by Father Zeng in the town of Fuzhou. The priest was standing in for Bishop Thomas Zeng Jingmu, of Yujiang.

December 2007: Reports showed acts of government oppression against an orphanage run by the 'Underground' Church in Wuqui, (Hebei province). The orphanage caters for hundreds of abandoned and often handicapped children. Local government has banned the orphanage from receiving donations and visits from local people. The local government has installed a video camera at the orphanage's entrance and Sisters have been interrogated at length by the police. During 2007, volunteers, some bringing gifts to the orphanage, were stopped by the police and fined. The Sisters belong to Zhengding diocese, whose Bishop, Julius Jia Zhiguo, continues to be arrested on a regular basis for repeatedly refusing to join the CCPA.[64]

May 2008: The Chinese authorities mounted a clampdown on a pilgrimage to Sheshan, near Shanghai, on 24th May, which Pope Benedict XVI announced as a Day of Prayer for China. Original estimates suggested a turn-out of 200,000 but in the event only 2,500 took part. To prevent them and their faithful taking part, 'Underground' Bishop Joseph Fan Zhongliang of Shanghai and his priests were tightly controlled and some were put under house arrest. The day before the pilgrimage, both 'Underground' and 'Official' priests from Zhengding (Hebei Province) were arrested. They were forced to "take a trip" with the police or stay in a hotel before being released shortly after the pilgrimage. Other priests were ordered "not to respond to the appeal of the Pope of Rome". Elsewhere in Taiyuan, Shaanxi province, the police closed a shrine as plans got underway for a similar pilgrimage on the same day. The police blocked the road to the shrine to stop the flow of pilgrims, who were forced to return home. Eye witnesses said police forces outnumbered the pilgrims. Meantime, Cardinal Joseph Zen Ze-kiun of Hong Kong was forced to cancel plans for 1,000 people in his diocese to take part in the Sheshan pilgrimage. In the event 80 people from Hong Kong went to Shanghai. Not only were they prevented from going to Sheshan but were banned from celebrating Mass in churches in Shanghai. One 'Underground' Catholic said the authorities "were blocking the Holy Father's instructions in any way they can".[65]

Profile: A Chinese Seminarian

Looking at him in his boots, cap and scruffy coat, it would be easy to mistake this man for a farm labourer, one of countless many in China. And in a sense it is true – he has just come from the fields where he has been helping farm labourers.

But it soon emerges that this is a seminarian from the 'Underground' community of the Catholic Church, for decades ruthlessly oppressed for its refusal to consent to registration by the Chinese authorities. Effectively outlawed as dissidents, many 'Underground' Catholics walk with danger every day of their lives. They suffer the pain of ongoing tension with the government-registered 'Official' Catholic Church.

Not that you would think it from this seminarian, who quickly launches into his life-story. Safe within the confines of his church and willing to speak – assuming key details are left out – the seminarian describes how he has spent more than a dozen years in training.

In that time, the attitudes of the authorities have totally changed. "When I first started, the government refused to accept 'Underground' seminarians," he declares. "We had to be scattered in different parishes to avoid detection. The organisation of it was very random and ad hoc. We had to be ready for a change at any moment."

"There were a lot of risks," he explains. "In the 1990s, when we came here, we studied philosophy in secret. We knew that if the government caught us, they would put us in prison."

And, to demonstrate the point, he describes how the authorities at one stage tracked the seminarians down to their secret location and chased them. "We had to jump over a wall and make a run for it," he explained. It all seems a long time ago. He adds: "Now, when I say I am a major seminarian, the authorities accept it."

Of course, this seminarian's story is far from representative of the situation across China. Again and again, observers of Church–State relations in China stress the massive differences in government policy, comparing one province, or district, with another.

And yet, this would-be priest's testimony shows how far things have come in some parts of the country.

More conciliatory they may be, but the authorities' continued oppression of the 'Underground' Church in China still leaves a big question mark over the seminarian's ordination.

He explained: "My ordination's been put back several times – I am not quite sure how many, in fact. The problem is that if my bishop ordains me, they won't recognise my priesthood because they don't recognise the bishop's ecclesiastical office."

He adds: "My bishop has repeatedly tried to get the Government's go-ahead for my ordination, but so far without success."

The seminarian tells how a few months earlier an 'Underground' bishop secretly ordained several priests, only for another bishop, this time from the 'Official' Church, to come along and preside at a repeat performance of the ceremony the very next day.

He adds: "It's a strange situation – difficult for outsiders to understand."

There is more pressure on the Church to push ahead with ordinations because vocations in many regions have begun to decline. The total number of seminarians in China – both 'Underground' and 'Official' combined – is still 1,500, but nationally new recruits have dwindled in number. One reason is China's One Child Policy; Catholic parents strongly oppose their precious off-spring giving their life away to the Church.

Also, it is a reflection of the growing materialism in Chinese society, which is creating a mass migration of people from the countryside to the towns – all in search of a decent living and the chance to send their child to school. But, as a country lad himself, this particular seminarian shows little sign of being distracted by material gain.

He said: "To be a priest is a wonderful thing. After more than a dozen years of often very hard training, ordination is just so important for me."

He adds: "People in China face huge challenges – both if they stay in the terrible poverty of the villages and also if they take the risk of moving to the city. There's a huge sense of uncertainty. They need to know Jesus Christ. They need someone to listen to them, to help them to find God."

30

Cuba

Population	Religions	Christian Population
11.3 million	Christian 44% Atheist 37% Animist 18% Other 1%	5 million

The tight controls on religious activity in Cuba are at last easing up nearly 50 years after Fidel Castro seized power and established the first communist regime in the Western Hemisphere. When in February 2008 Fidel formally ceded power to Raúl, his brother and long-standing right-hand man, it coincided with a visit to Cuba by Vatican Secretary of State Cardinal Tarcisio Bertone, an event marking the 10th anniversary of Pope John Paul II's historic journey to the island. During his visit, Cardinal Bertone unveiled a statue of John Paul II in Santa Clara and had discussions with the new president. The trip resurrected hopes of a new spring-time in Christian life and practice in Cuba, building on the legacy of the former Pope.

For decades, Church authorities have experienced insuperable difficulties obtaining permits to build and repair churches and other religious structures. The authorities repeatedly turned down requests for foreign priests and Sisters to work in Cuba. Access to the media is still tightly controlled and surveillance of religious activities continues. The impact of communism has been huge but although practice of Christianity is comparatively rare, many people still regard themselves as Catholics.

Despite the signs of progress, some key obstacles hamper the Church's full recovery from the crackdown Fidel instrumented in the early 1960s. The regime continues to refuse to hand back Church buildings seized in 1961. Other Christian denominations have also suffered. Many of these problems remain but even before Raúl came to power, change was in the air. In 2006, during Raúl Castro's temporary rule, Cardinal Jaime Ortega, the Archbishop of Havana, publically announced that he would pray that God would enlighten the new government.[66] It is a far cry from the not so distant past when the most a Cuban prelate felt able to pray for was the Church's survival.

2007: Following a relaxation in government controls, more than 90 public processions took place during the year at the national shrine of Our Lady of Charity of Cobre, Santiago de Cuba, south-east Cuba. The shrine recalls how, in the 17th century, fishermen discovered an image of the Virgin floating towards them on the water.[67]

Summer 2007: The ordinary assembly of CELAM (Bishops' Conference of Latin America) was held for the first time in Cuba. Attending the meeting, the 31st of its kind, were Cuban vice presidents Carlos Lage and Esteban Lazo. The bishops agreed on the need to encourage Latin American professionals in Cuba to promote social and human values.[68]

April 2007: Jorge Luis Garcia Perez 'Antuñez', a Cuban political prisoner and a committed Christian, was released from jail after serving 17 years for his opposition to the Castro regime. Pope John Paul II appealed for the release of 'Antuñez' during his visit to Cuba in 1998.[69]

June 2007: The family of a jailed Catholic doctor expressed serious concerns for his health. He was reported to have lost 5½ stone while suffering from chronic diarrhoea and malnutrition. Other prisoners reported that he had been given mind-altering drugs. On one occasion, he had been seen crying incessantly and banging his head against a wall. The previous September, he was badly beaten by a fellow prisoner. The Christian Liberation Movement blamed the beating on the government for housing political prisoners together with common criminals, many of whom had committed violent offences. Government doctors told his family he needed urgent surgery after discovering a cyst in his kidneys. But his family feared he would not survive the surgery.[70]

December 2007: 200 police and communist militants forcibly removed about 20 dissidents gathered outside the presbytery of Santa Teresita, in south-east Cuba. The parish priest and the Archbishop of Santiago de Cuba later received an apology.[71]

February 2008: Vatican Secretary of State Cardinal Tarcisio Bertone opened the first completely new church building approved by the authorities in recent times – a bishop's house for the new Diocese of Guantanamo. Until then, Catholic leaders had only received permission to repair existing Church buildings.[72]

Profile: Bishop Arturo González from Cuba

Monsignor Arturo González Amador took office as Bishop of Santa Clara in summer 1999, aged only 43. Here he discusses his life and work in a region which for years has been important for sugar-cane production. Extract from an ACN interview in Rome, May 2008.

"I try to be a father in body and soul to all those who are near me. The father-bishop of Santa Clara diocese is the same as any other priest. He makes sure that he is attentive to the problems of his children, to make his joys, the joys of his children and to make his successes, those of his children. He tries to accompany them spiritually in all manner of circumstances; to be by their side and to do all that a father should do; to watch over them before God and to watch over them before the world too.

"They are people who always give me comfort and I feel deeply comforted by their way of being. On occasion, I wish they were a little better than they are – why not say it! – but they are good people, endearing, simple; they are near to me; they work closely with me.

"The conferences given by John Paul II [during his January 1998 visit to the island] are unforgettable to the Cuban people. And I don't only mean Catholics but the whole Cuban people. They were days when a completely different language was used, where the expression of brotherhood and fraternity came naturally and was not forced. It was a time of happiness, of joy, of freedom. They were unforgettable days in the lives of the people and in the life of the Church.

"Pope John Paul's visit left its mark on the lives of the people, and the Church. This is indisputable. The Pope managed to bring the Church to the middle of the square. He gave the Church public recognition and made it gain ground. The Church discovered that it had the Word that the people were waiting to hear. And it is on this foundation that we have worked over

33

the past 10 years. Our work has been inspired by John Paul II; his was a drive of evangelisation, a drive of charity and of closeness to the people, a drive that promotes human development, putting a grain of sand towards building the kingdom. They were amazing days, when the Church reached out to rural areas where its presence had never been felt. This is what the Pope has left us – a pastoral programme – enabling us move forwards.

"The Cuban Church's main area of work is primarily vocational formation, human and Christian formation. Most importantly the Cuban people need human guidance. And in second place, they need financial support through charity. In Cuba many people need charity but not only material charity. They also need that word of guidance, of advice, of encouragement; that is to say, physical and spiritual support. It's not enough 'to give, give, give', but the people also need to be taught how to think, how to manage their lives, and they need to be taught how to find new ways of living. That is the work of the Church.

"The Cuban Church is a small Church; it is a minority. The majority of people declare themselves to be Catholic. A lot of them say to me: 'Do you know me? I am a Catholic.' 'Well, I certainly have never seen you at Mass.' He recognises himself as a Catholic; he baptises his children; he shows a great devotion to the Sacred Heart of Jesus and to Our Lady of Charity [Cuban Marian devotion]. Overnight in 1961 the Church was stripped of all its means of support, its charitable work, its schools, etc. The Church was reduced – and I can say this in all certainty – to a shadow of its former self. From this point on, the Church was there to support the people, to make Her own life, the life of the people and to be near the people with Her doors always open to welcome the people.

"In the last few years, and especially as a result of John Paul II's visit, the Church has succeeded in bringing in new priests, new religious congregations. We have promoted vocations [to the priesthood]. All of this has enabled us to count on the support of the religious as well as the lay people. The lay people are extremely committed; theirs is a community in which we have invested a lot of formation; it is a community that accepts responsibility and cooperates well in the task of evangelisation. They are our right hand and our left hand."

Egypt

Population	Religions	Christian Population
75.5 million	Muslim 93.5% Christian 6% Other 0.5%	4.5 million

The rise of the Brotherhood of Islam, an extremist Islamic movement, has put increasing pressure on Christians in Egypt. The country has the largest Christian population in the Middle East – more than four million. Despite their large number, Christians – made up mostly of Coptic Orthodox – are reduced to second class citizens and have limited freedom of worship.

Amid increasing poverty and anti-West sentiment, especially since the start of the US-led 'War on Terror', Muslim fundamentalist groups have become a lightning rod for disaffected communities, polling nearly 20 percent of the vote in recent elections. Claiming that President Hosni Mubarak's regime is too pro-West, such groups have pushed for the full introduction of *Shari'a* Islamic law and further steps to reduce non-Muslim influences across the country.

Despite officially upholding religious freedom, the constitution insists on *Shari'a* as the principal source of legislation. In practice, the problem is worse still: Christians have been officially banned from building new churches, although loop-holes are sometimes found. When local Muslims discover the plans, they frequently build a mosque nearby or beat up local Christians close to where the new church is to be built.

Mandatory identity cards state a person's religion, increasing the risk of discrimination at school or in the workplace. In many schools, for example, it is not permissible for a Christian to be top of the class. Coptic Christians are not allowed to teach Arabic except in small classes where it is taught without using the *Qur'an*.

There have been increased reports of Christian girls as young as 14 being kidnapped to marry Muslims. Christians are barred from positions of power. There has been a rise in cases of alleged police inaction to stamp out crimes against Christian communities. This particularly applies to 'revenge' attacks by Islamists in response to minor incidents involving Christians, e.g. throwing stones at a Christian home after a Christian teenager inadvertently knocked a Muslim child off his bicycle.

But there have been some signs of progress. For many years, Muslims converting to Christianity have been accused of apostasy and have been forced to flee the country to escape possible murder. A break-through came in February 2008 when Egypt's supreme court authorised 12 Coptic Orthodox to revert to Christianity even though at some point they had become Muslim. The Christians' lawyers upheld the verdict as "a victory for freedom of religion in Egypt". For many Christians, increasingly fed up with being treated poorly, such an outcome provides a glimmer of hope.

2007: The UN's International Labour Office produced a report revealing discrimination in schools and colleges. "One of the most resilient forms of discrimination involves the targeting of Coptic [Christians] in Egypt, who are denied equal access to education and equal opportunities in recruitment and promotion."[73]

April 2007: Bishop Youhannes Zakaria of Luxor (Thebes of ancient times) warned of the dangers of the Brotherhood of Islam, an extremist political movement which he said was becoming more influential. Warning of the party's increasing popularity at the polls, he indicated that its rise to power would have disastrous consequences for the country's Christian population, because of its determination to introduce *Shari'a* and reduce non-Muslim influences. "The government is very afraid of the Brotherhood," said the bishop. "The government is concerned for its own survival."[74]

May 2007: In the village of Bamha, just south of Cairo, a group of Muslims looted and set fire to homes and shops owned by Coptic Christians. They responded to news from their imam that the 'infidels' were enlarging their church, plans for which the Christians had obtained official permission.[75]

June 2007: In Zawyet Abdel-Qader, a city to the west of Alexandria, a number of Muslims attacked two Coptic Orthodox churches, looted shops owned by Christians and injured seven Christians. The attack was followed four days later by another attack in the same region against the Church of Our Lady, in Dekheila, also west of Alexandria.

June 2007: In Saft Meydoum, in the governorship of Beni Souwef, the parents of a young Muslim girl, who had been knocked down by a Coptic Christian on a bicycle, attacked the home of a Christian family, one of whom they believed was responsible. They threw stones at the building doing severe damage.[76]

August 2007: Adel Fawzi and Peter Ezzat (members of the Organisation of Near East Christians) were imprisoned on a charge of "attacking Islam" and "denominational sedition". They were found guilty of being partly responsible for the conversion of Mohamed Hegazy, who earlier that year asked for his change of religion to be registered officially. Aged 25, he had waited nine years to achieve his wish. After his conversion was made public, the rector of *El Azhar* University issued a *fatwa* (religious decree) accusing Hegazy of apostasy. He pronounced a death sentence both on him and his wife, Zeinab. She had also become Christian, taking the name Katrina. Her father told the Egyptian press: "I want the judges to make her divorce him and I want her sent back to me, alive or dead."

February 2008: The administrative Supreme Court authorised 12 Copts who had converted to Islam to return to their original faith. The lawyer representing the Copts said the decision set a precedent for the 457 similar appeals still pending in various administrative courts around the country.

May 2008: According to local sources, one Muslim was killed and four Christians were wounded in a clash over disputed land near a Christian monastery in central Egypt. The violence broke out after Christians in the town of Mallawy, south of Cairo, began constructing a wall around disputed land near Abu Fana monastery.[77]

June 2008: Bishop Antonios Aziz Mina of Guizeh called on Christians to show love and friendship even in the face of the recent attacks against Christians. He blamed poverty and ignorance for the rise in violence and extremism, which he said was aimed, at least in part, at Christians. He warned of massive emigration, which he said could only be reduced by aid from outside. He said the people believed "nowhere could be worse than their own country."[78]

Eritrea

Population	Religions	Christian Pop.
5 million	Muslim 50% Orthodox 40% Catholic 5% Protestant 2%, Other 3%	2.3 million

In the last few years, there has been an unrelenting clampdown on religious groups all over the country. Christians of all denominations have suffered gravely in an increasingly ruthless government campaign of intimidation against Churches of all kinds.

Much has changed since 2002 when state recognition was granted to the Eritrean Orthodox Church, the Catholic Church, the Evangelical Church (Lutherans) and Islam. Falling well short of government approval, the regulations under which the recognised religions operated required them to make a complete declaration of financial resources and possessions.

Unregistered religious groups faced ruthless persecution – incarceration and violence. But since 2004, the regime's efforts to silence unrecognised religions have begun to spread to recently approved religions. On 5th March 2004 President Isaias Afewerki declared a zero-tolerance policy towards religious groups guilty of "distancing [citizens] from the unity of the Eritrean people and [who] distort the real meaning of religion".

The regime, destabilised by the continuing stand-off with neighbouring Ethiopia, was losing patience with religious groups and its wrath peaked when it deposed Eritrean Orthodox Patriarch Antonios. As leader of the country's largest religious community, the Patriarch's summary dismissal shocked the nation. The government then proceeded to put him under house arrest and appoint a layman as administrator of the Church. Some months later, Bishop Dioskoros Mendefera succeeded as Patriarch. There were reports of widespread government interference in the synod.

Meanwhile, the Catholic Church's refusal to comply with government demands to release clergy for military service were met with a firm riposte: orders requiring the Church to hand over schools, clinics and other welfare operations. At the same time, persecution against non-registered religious groups got worse. With widespread reports of arrests of clergy and other religious figures and lengthy detention without charge, the US State Department has added Eritrea to its list of "countries of particular concern".

January 2007: The government arrested eight members of the Medhane Alem congregation, a renewal movement of the Coptic Orthodox Church. After their arrest in Keren (the regional capital of the Anseba Region), they were interrogated and asked to provide names of other members of the group. The government accused the Medhane Alem of "heresy" and wanting to "destroy" the Eritrean Orthodox Church. Three priests were arrested in 2006 and were subsequently imprisoned for at least two years.[79]

March 2007: Eritrea's Catholic bishops announced their refusal to comply with government demands for clergy to carry out military service. Alone in their defiance among religious leaders, the bishops cited Church law in their opposition to the scheme for clergy under the age of 50 to serve as soldiers rather than as chaplains. Church leaders stressed their concerns at the government's refusal to impose a time-limit on the conscription period.[80]

April 2007: The Synod of the Eritrean Orthodox Church "unanimously appointed" Dioskoros Mendefera as Patriarch to replace Patriarch Antonios, who had been placed under house arrest. Rumours of government intervention in the election soon spread, with Christian Solidarity Worldwide (CSW) calling Dioskoros a "renegade" appointed "16 months after the illegal deposition of the legal patriarch". CSW went on to condemn the government for an act of "interference of unprecedented seriousness". By then, reports emerged that the authorities had forcibly taken Patriarch Antonios' robes and insignia and that he was being denied communion. Antonios is still acknowledged as the legitimate leader of the Eritrean Orthodox Church by Patriarch Shenoudah III, leader of the Coptic Orthodox Church.

April 2007: Following an in-depth investigation, *Aid to the Church in Need* produced a report giving a damning verdict on religious freedom in Eritrea. The report said the government had demanded Church leaders submit a comprehensive list of clergy, their ages and whereabouts. The Church refused to cooperate, stating that the demand was linked to the government's order for clergy to carry out military service. The ACN report goes on to spell out the worsening poverty of the country and how the Church was providing a "rare glimmer of hope" providing welfare support for the young and infirm. ACN reported that despite the fact that

39

there were only 200,000 Catholics in Eritrea, there were nearly 80 diocesan seminarians and more than 60 novice Franciscans.[81]

May 2007: 20 members of the Kaile Hiwot Church were arrested together with their children in Dekemhare, 20 miles south of the capital, Asmara. On 1st January 2008, Kaile Hiwot pastor Michael Abraha was also arrested after the authorities confiscated a video showing him officiating at a wedding. He was released a month later. A few months previously, another Kaile Hiwot minister was arrested, having already spent 10 months in solitary confinement after being reported for attending a Christian wedding. In September 2007, the government demanded that the Kale Hiwot Church surrender all its property and assets to the government. The order specifically applied to the Church's relief work, including church buildings, schools and vehicles. The order came almost a year after security forces raided and closed down the central offices of the Kale Hiwot Church. At the time, a source close to the Church said: "This is a direct attack upon the Church."[82]

August 2007: The authorities ordered the Catholic Church to hand over to the Ministry for Social Welfare and Labour schools, clinics, orphanages and educational centres for women. The following day, the country's four bishops sent a letter refusing to cooperate, and asserting the Church's right to deny government interference in internal structures and matters of faith and practice.

September 2007: Evangelical Christian Mogos Solom Semere died in the Adi-Nefase army camp near Assab, a coastal city in the south-east. He had been in prison since 2001 for being a member of a non-recognised Protestant Church. His death "was the consequence of physical torture and chronic pneumonia, for which he had been denied appropriate medical care".[83]

September 2007: The Eritrean government was accused of torturing to death Nigsti Haile, aged 33, at the Wi'a Military Training Centre, 20 miles from the sea port of Massawa. She was one of 10 single Christian women arrested at a church gathering in Keren. She was allegedly killed for refusing to sign a letter recanting her faith.[84]

October 2007: Helen Berhane, an Eritrean singer of Christian songs imprisoned and tortured for two years before managing to escape, was given political asylum in Denmark. As reported by *BBC News*, the singer, who was a member of the unauthorised Evangelical Rema Church, was arrested on 13th May 2004, after recording and selling a cassette of Christian hymns. For two years she was imprisoned in a metal container in the Mai Serwa prison camp near Asmara, and often beaten to make her recant. After a widespread international campaign, she was released at the end of October 2006. Having regained her freedom, she immediately fled to Sudan, where she was given asylum. A few months later, she was welcomed by Denmark. She now uses a wheelchair because of the serious injuries inflicted on her legs and feet while she was in prison.

November 2007: The government deported 11 Catholic missionaries from a range of nationalities – both Sisters and priests – after refusing to renew their residency permits. According to the Habeisha Agency, the missionaries "have always contributed to the progress and development of our country and hence by expelling them, the regime has committed an extremely uncivilised act, damaging the population. By doing this, the regime wishes to intimidate the Catholic hierarchy."

June 2008: Egypt opened fire on Eritrean refugees entering the country and forcibly deported more than 1,000 of them – many of whom were Christians fleeing Eritrea's restrictions on religious practice. After Israel was inundated by "a tsunami" of Sudanese and Eritrean refugees arriving via Egypt, Egypt was asked to intervene. However, instead of providing sanctuary for the refugees, it began shooting and forcibly deporting them. 16 refugees were shot in the first six months of 2008. Egypt forcibly deported 1,000 Eritrean refugees. The Eritrean Democratic Alliance (EDA) – the exiled opposition party – condemned the deportations. The EDA said they had confirmation that a number of refugees returned to Eritrea were being sent to secret prisons, tortured to death, or "shot dead in front of their colleagues to terrorise others from further attempts of escape". *Amnesty International* has documented how torture is being inflicted on Eritreans imprisoned for their faith and has appealed to Western governments to stop the repatriation of Eritrean refugees. According to the EDA, Libya is also preparing to deport hundreds of Eritreans.[85]

India

Population	Religions	Christian Population	
1.1 billion	Hindu 80% Muslim 14% Christian 2% Sikh 2%, Other 2%	22 million	

Christmas celebrations descended into catastrophe when Hindu fanatics went on the rampage in the Indian state of Orissa. Altogether 70 churches and other Christian institutions were attacked and 600 Christian homes were destroyed. The unprovoked attack at the end of 2007 was a wake-up call to the plight of Christians in parts of the country and demonstrated to Indians that a new phase of extremism was now under way.

Although Article 25 of the constitution guarantees individuals the right to choose their religion, 'anti-conversion' laws are in force in many states. The laws impose an average jail term of four years as well as a hefty fine for people guilty of "activities related to conversion". Similar laws are in place in states including Orissa, Tamil Nadu, Chhattisgarh, Arunachal Pradesh, Gujarat and Madhya Pradesh. When the government over-ruled the law's introduction in Tamil Nadu, the intervention was ignored by the local authorities.

In Madhya Pradesh all prospective converts must sign a document before a district judge declaring their wish to change religion at least a month before the ceremony. Failure to comply risks a fine of up to 1,000 rupees and imprisonment. Police must "verify the credentials of the priest or organisation" before the conversion and should be satisfied that it is "not being done by force or with allurement". Ministers must inform the authorities of their intention to preside over conversion ceremonies. They should also provide the name and address of the convert and the date of the ceremony – or be fined 5,000 rupees and face a year's imprisonment.

Christian schools are targets for violence. In 2007, the Catholic Church reported over 100 episodes of violence against Christian institutions or staff, down from 215 the previous year. In many cases, the schools are warned of impending attacks.

Regional governments have adopted plans to help Dalits (so-called 'untouchables') overcome centuries of inferior social status but Christian Dalits are often refused aid. In some states, such as Jharkhand, the authorities tried to avoid helping them by reclassifying Dalits as members of the Christian minority.

In Chhattisgarh state the government has seized the Catholic Church's property on the pretext of insisting that it be returned to its rightful tribal owners. In Jashpur diocese alone there are hundreds of cases pending against tribal Christians accused of giving land to the Church. In Andhra Pradesh, authorities banned non-Hindus from Hindu holy places. Since 23rd July 2007 a state law has banned other religions from holding activities close to Hindu sacred places.

Sajan K. George, chairman of the Global Council of Indian Christians, said that his organisation had "collected documentary evidence of more than 500 reported cases of anti-Christian violence" that took place "all over the country" between January 2006 and November 2007, largely the work of extremists such as the *Bharatiya Janata Party* (BJP).

January 2007: An 18-year-old Christian convert from Hinduism died four days after he was found lying wounded near a railway track in Madhya Pradesh. It is alleged he was pushed out of a train by Hindu extremists.[86]

March 2007: Protestant Pastor Reginald Howell was beaten with steel bars as he prayed with disabled people in Hanumangarh (Rajasthan). Doctors refused to treat him fearing retaliation from the fanatics. Police refused to accept the complaint filed by Pastor Howell and forced him to leave the state and return to his home town in neighbouring Punjab.

May 2007: Father George Minj was beaten by unidentified assailants near Ranchi (Jharkhand). Sister Teresa Kindo, who was with him at the time, was also injured.

June 2007: Youths beat up Protestant Pastor Laxmi Narayan Gowda, in Hessarghatta (Karnataka state), parading him naked in the streets of nearby Bangalore. They put a sign around his neck that read: "I am the one who was converting people." They then tried to set him on fire.[87]

August 2007: Extremists in Chitradurga district (Karnataka) handed out flyers ordering Christians to leave India, "or return to the mother religion which is Hinduism" or be killed. The flyer listed their crimes, including

43

"treating everyone with love, educating orphans in order to convert them, offering health care to those who cannot afford it, ignoring the caste system, accepting marriage by consent, and agreeing to commercial exchanges between people who should not even associate with each other".

October 2007: Vipin Mandloli, 27, an Evangelical convert from Hinduism, died from gunshot wounds near the village of Aamkut (Madhya Pradesh). Sajan K. George of the Global Council of Indian Christians, said that three Hindu priests had offered Mr Mandloli's life to their goddess, Kalì.

October 2007: In Raseli (Madhya Pradesh), five Claretian nuns were beaten with sticks by activists from the *Dharma Raksha Samiti* (Religion Protection Council), an extremist group which supports *sati* (suttee), the ritual suicide of widowed Hindu women.

November 2007: Hindu fundamentalists attacked the Pentecostal church in the village of Mandwa, Jagdalpur district (Chhattisgarh). Those inside were tied up and beaten; Pastor Sudroo died from the injuries he received. The attackers eventually set the church on fire. Police did not investigate the incident.

December 2007: Dozens of people were hurt and many others were killed when Hindu extremists attacked Christian homes, churches and other buildings in Orissa state, eastern India. Altogether 70 churches and other church buildings were attacked, destroyed or set on fire; 600 Christian homes were damaged or destroyed. Altogether 5,000 people were affected in some way. The incident began when fundamentalists forcibly removed Christmas decorations erected with the permission of the authorities. Following protests by the Christians, more than 200 extremists attacked them with clubs, swords, and rifles. On Christmas Day, the attackers returned in force and destroyed churches in the village of Bamunigam. They also attacked and burned the homes of the Christians. The violence spread elsewhere. Two people were gunned down by security forces when Christians took to the streets to protest against the attacks.

February 2008: In Kosmi, near Balaghat, a mob of Hindu extremists dragged at least four people from a home where Christians were meeting and beat them with bamboo poles, rods and belts, yelling: "Stop conversions."[88]

March 2008: Peerzada Shakeel, a convert to Christianity from Islam, was arrested along with his wife Arifa on 26th March on trumped-up charges of forced conversions. A few days earlier, on 21st March (Good Friday), members of the local mosque broke into his house and beat Shakeel, asking him why he was not saying Islamic prayers. They dragged him to the mosque and when he told them he would only worship Christ, they hit him again. The charges against Shakeel were brought by his father, local mosque member Peerzada Gulam Nabi. Shakeel and his wife were arrested and taken to a police station in Srinagar, Kashmir. Although released on bail on 27th March they were placed under house arrest.[89]

March 2008: Hindu radicals attacked two Catholic nuns and three teenage girls as they prepared to hold a women's educational programme. The extremists shouted at the nuns, accusing them of "converting tribal people to Christianity". According to Sister Tuscano, the mob "told us to leave the village at once and never to come back or else they would break our legs." The programme's activities include running adult literacy classes, helping to set up self-help groups and Aids awareness classes.[90]

May 2008: A mob armed with iron rods and wooden clubs attacked a Christian pastor named Rampal Kori on his way home from an all-night vigil near Maoganj village, about five miles from Dadar, Mumbai. The mob angrily questioned him about the vigil. They accused him of forcibly converting the villagers to Christianity before beating him with an iron rod. Pastor Rampal fell down, bleeding heavily, as his attackers warned him against holding Christian worship again. They stole 3,000 rupees from the pastor and kicked him before leaving him semi-conscious.[91]

May 2008: A group of 20 people completely destroyed the thatched church in Tembi village, Andhra Pradesh.[92]

July 2008: An orphanage and a parish church in Orissa were looted and destroyed in an attack by the Sangh Parivar Hindu fundamentalist group. Archbishop Raphael Cheenath of Cuttack-Bhubaneshwar said, "There are about a million Christians in Orissa and the Cross of Christ is firmly planted in the state – no persecution can eliminate it."[93]

Indonesia

Population	Religions	Christian Population
231.5 million	Muslim 86% Christian 8.5% Hindu 2% Other 3.5%	20 million

Religious liberty is increasingly under threat from an intense campaign of Islamization masterminded by extremist movements which the government often struggles to control. Aceh remains the only province authorised to apply *Shari'a* Islamic law. But in other regions, there was in 2006-07 a sharp rise in new local laws inspired by Islamic precepts. According to the *Indonesian Women's Coalition*, there were at least 46 such laws by the spring of 2008. In some areas the laws have been extended to non-Muslims. As yet, central government, based in the capital, Jakarta, seems to have done little to keep its promise of opposing the new laws.

Since 2004, dozens of districts and municipalities have adopted laws influenced by *Shari'a*. Strong protests took place when a woman walking home by herself after night-fall was accused of prostitution under a 2005 law passed by the Tangerang region. A law proposed in 2007 by the Justice and Peace Party to apply *Shari'a* to all residents in Aceh province regardless of their religion sparked serious objections. A ruling, due to be imposed in 2008 in Western Sumatra, established a test in reading and writing the *Qur'an* for both primary and high school students. The declaration, which also applied to couples wishing to marry, apparently made no allowances for non-Muslims.[94]

Christians are often accused of proselytism. In April 2007, the so-called Islamic Division accused the Pasudan Christian Church in Bandung, West Java province, of paying local Muslims to convert to Christianity. Across the province, since 2005 there has been a dramatic rise in extremist violence against Christian communities, especially house churches. They have been threatened with enforced closure after Church leaders were denied permits for the buildings to act as places of worship. Permissions for new religious buildings are still denied in many areas. Islamic extremist groups and local authorities closed 110 churches from 2004 to 2007.[95]

June 2007: Up to 150 Islamic extremists marched to Bandung demanding the closure of private homes being used as churches.

July 2007: Over 1,000 Muslims protested against the existence of the Carmelite prayer centre on Cikanyere Hill in Kota Bunga (West Java), about 100 kilometres from Jakarta. When the Carmelite centre started planning a conference on the Holy Trinity, a group called the Islamic People of Cianjur held a protest, setting off from the Siti Hajar Mosque, less than a mile away. They were joined by Muslims from nearby towns.

September 2007: At least 300 Islamic extremists attacked a house church in Tangerang regency, near Jakarta. The pastor and six faithful were badly hurt. They also destroyed all the community's possessions. The attack took place while the church of about 60 people were holding Sunday worship.

November 2007: A mob attacked a house church in Dayeuh Kolot sub-district as people were about to hold Sunday Service at the home of Pastor Obertina. Police eventually arrived, dispersing the crowd. The pastor said services had been held in her home since the 1980s without any complaints.

December 2007: Authorities prevented the parish priest of Christ's Peace Church in South Duri, West Jakarta, from celebrating Mass. It was the final act in a drama effectively leading to the church's enforced closure. The sub-district of Tambura had ordered a halt to all activities at the church to avoid "social tensions". Although he signed a document agreeing to most of the requests, the parish priest, Father Matthew Widyalestari, asked to continue celebrating Sunday Mass for his 4,000 parishioners. Finally, on 7th December, the political authorities insisted that he should not celebrate Mass because of concerns about "public order".

February 2008: The congregation of Love Evangelical Bethel Church on Sumatra Island ceased Sunday services after about 60 demonstrators from four local mosques demanded the church's closure. The demonstrators said the church did not have a permit to expand. It is the only church in a village which has 14 mosques, none of which have permits. The church is registered with local Religious Affairs' authorities.[96]

June 2008: Members of the Islamic Defenders' Front in Tangerang (Banten province) threatened to kill Baptist leader Bedali Hulu when he visited his elderly mother-in-law. The church, which meets in people's homes, has received many threats.[97]

47

Iran

Population	Religions	Christian Population
71 million	Shi'a Muslim 89% Sunni Muslim 9% Other 2%	200,000

Amid increasing international alarm, Iran's President Mahmoud Ahmadinejad has pressed ahead with inculcating 'revolutionary' ideas into the life-blood of this, the world's main *Shia* Muslim nation. The state has progressively enforced a hard-line and uncompromising vision of Islam that puts increasing pressures on minority groups. In February 2008, parliament debated a bill imposing the death sentence on "apostates", Muslims who change their faith.

Nearly 30 years after Ayatollah Khomeini seized power, *Shia* Islam truly permeates Iran. Article 4 of the constitution declares that the country's laws and institutions "must be based on Islamic criteria". 'Modesty patrols' enforce Islamic dress codes which apply to everyone, including non-Muslims. For women, this means no make-up, cutting their hair short, using a head veil and wearing long loose garments, usually the chandor.

Domestic censorship is increasing. Under President Ahmadinejad, 'revolutionary' ideas are at work in the running of everything from the traffic police to the fire service. In addition to 'modesty patrols', he has started a campaign against immorality, cracking down on dissident trade unionists, intellectuals, journalists, etc. In practice this amounts to an attack on Internet and satellite TV use. Although relatively few dissidents – including Nobel Peace Prize laureate Shirin Ebadi – have been jailed, their freedom is severely curtailed.

Christians are an officially recognised minority. Although they are classified as *dhimmi,* meaning 'protected', in practice Christians are second class citizens and are open to abuse and denied many rights. Both the Eastern (Armenian and Chaldean) and Latin rite Catholic Churches are permitted to hold services in churches and other buildings designated for the purpose but they are forbidden from expressing their faith in public.

The Latin Church is made up mostly of expatriates living in the capital, Teheran, including diplomats and students. Close ties to foreign embassies provide a legal basis for the community's existence, including its places of worship and burial. Protestant communities are backed by various foreign embassies and are respected as Christian, but their status remains precarious. House churches have become particular targets for the regime.

Although President Ahmadinejad has boasted that the Christian minority "enjoys equal rights", any public expression of faith or missionary action, whatever form it may take, is banned as proselytism. Although officially deployed to "protect" Christian places of worship, police are present at Christian religious services, in effect banning all those who are not "legally Christian" from attending.

Christians are also marginalised by persistent undercounting. According to official government statistics, there are only 79,000 Christians in the country. However, the Armenian Orthodox alone number up to 200,000 and other Christian denominations have at least 20,000 members.

January 2007: Iran's secret police launched raids against Christian communities in Karaj, Teheran, Rasht and Bandar-i-Anzali, arresting 15 members of the Free Evangelical movement. Agents gave several reasons for the arrests, including evangelisation and acts against national security. Most of the Christians were released except for Evangelical leader Behrouz Sadegh-Khandjani. He remained in police custody in Teheran, allegedly because he had not paid for damages relating to an accident with an uninsured rental car.[98]

February 2008: The Iranian parliament tabled a bill that would impose the death penalty for "apostates" from Islam. Under current rules, Muslims who change faith risk receiving the death penalty but so far international pressure has prevented Islamic courts from imposing it. Instead the sentence is usually commuted to imprisonment.[99]

May 2008: Over the course of several weeks at least 12 converts to Christianity were arrested and detained by Iranian police. They were held in undisclosed locations. This was the latest in a series of arrests of Christians during 2008. Reports show that during detention, converts were asked to renounce their faith and were only released after signing documents obliging them to cease evangelistic activities.

Iraq

Population	Religions	Christian Population
29 million	Shi'a Muslim 60% Sunni Muslim 37% Other 3%	300,000

The kidnapping and death of Archbishop Paulos Faraj Rahho in early 2008 shocked the world into recognising that there was one aspect of the Iraq crisis that had been almost completely ignored; the country's ancient Church was now in the grip of persecution, with potentially fatal consequences. The assaults against Iraqi Christians were now as bloody as they were unrelenting.

The 800,000-strong Christian community in Iraq at the turn of the millennium had suffered more than its fair share of knocks under Saddam Hussein's regime, not least in the 1988 Kurdish massacres. But they had survived intact and tentatively looked forward to life after the Baathist regime.

For a time, in the initial aftermath of the 2003 invasion, such hopes looked set to be realised but all that was soon to change. Sporadic attacks against Christian individuals, shops and other businesses soon grew into a wider and more co-ordinated assault on the Church's very presence in this, the Biblical Cradle of Christianity.

The attacks on five churches in Baghdad and Mosul, in north-west Iraq, on 1st August 2004, marked the start of what soon became a sustained campaign by militia to flush out all traces of Christian influence. What had started out as one community's share of the pain and misery suffered by everyone regardless of religion, class or tribe, had now become a nightmare unique in its intensity and bloodshed. Nor have the steps to rebuild the civil structures in Iraq offered any meaningful protection to the Christian community.

The constitution approved on 15th October 2005 guaranteed political, cultural and educational rights for all religions (Articles 2.1b and 2.2) but significantly, at the same time, proclaimed Islam as the "official religion". It declared: "No law can be passed that contradicts the undisputed rules of Islam." (Article 2.1a)[100]

Senior clergy argued that the predominance of *Shari'a* negated the value of apparently important steps forward for the Church – including the unprecedented decision to allow political parties for Christians and the return of schools to the Church decades after they were nationalised by Saddam. In any case, as violence erupted across Iraq, such questions became increasingly irrelevant.

It soon emerged that key regions of Iraq, most notably Baghdad, were being carved up by Islamist militia, both *Shi'a* and *Sunni*, each vying for supremacy. The only thing they seemed able to agree on was the urgent need to stamp out Christianity. Reports soon started filtering through of militia forces conducting house-to-house searches for Christians. Those they found were given the ultimatum of either converting to Islam or facing retribution. The options included eviction from their homes and paying vast fines in accordance with Islamic *Jizya* taxation.

In some instances, threats were made for Christian women to be handed over to become wives to militia chiefs. Each month, Christians were pouring over Iraq's borders. By the summer of 2008, it was estimated that altogether there were 200,000 Iraqi Christian refugees in Jordan and Syria plus several thousand more in Turkey, Lebanon and Egypt. The Christian population in Iraq meanwhile had plummeted to less than 350,000.

Many of those still left in the country had fled north, leaving Basra and other major urban areas formerly home to many thousands of Christians. Amid signs that Iraq was now breaking down into different factions, the Kurdish north was attracting many displaced Christians. Reports in June 2008 showed there were up to 50,000 alone in northern Iraq, including the Nineveh plains in the north-west outside the city of Mosul.

The crisis came to a head in June 2007 with the assassination of Mosul's Father Ragheed Ganni, aged only 34, and three of his sub-deacons. It was an atrocity equalled only by the death of their bishop, Paulos Faraj Rahho, barely nine months later. By the summer of 2008, Archbishop Louis Sako of Kirkuk was warning the West of "the gravity of the tragedy of the Iraqi Christians", adding: "They are the most ancient inhabitants of the country but they are often the victims of violence that is aimed at them because they are Christians. Iraqi Christians feel alone, isolated and forgotten."[101]

51

January 2007: An ACN project assessment trip to northern Iraq (Kurdistan), Ankawa and Kirkuk revealed the desperation and suffering of tens of thousands of Christians swarming into the region after being displaced from their homes in the south. The trip's findings were very different to those of the previous one, in June 2003, weeks after the overthrow of Saddam. The 2007 ACN report stated: "Just after Saddam went, there were so many signs of hope – now people feel they can only turn to God for help." The document concluded with the need for massive support for displaced Christians as well as Babel Theological and Philosophical College and St Peter's Seminary, both evacuated from Baghdad the previous summer and now in the north. The students were found to be living in portacabins and suffering a dire shortage of study materials and classrooms.[102]

May 2007: Muslims on the rampage in al-Dora, south-west Baghdad, set fire to St. George's Assyrian Orthodox Church.

May 2007: Church leaders confirmed the release of Chaldean priest Father Nawzat Hanna, 38, three days after he was kidnapped. His captors had demanded a huge ransom but a negotiated settlement was reached.

May 2007: Church leaders reported a major assault by Muslim fundamentalists in Baghdad's al-Dora district, whose strong Christian presence earned the district the nickname the 'Vatican of Iraq'. During spring 2007, bishops said up to 1,000 Christians had been forced from their homes in al-Dora.
Extremist Muslims went from house-to-house looking for Christians. Those they found were told to convert to Islam. Those who refused risked eviction from their homes, or a *Jizya* tax payment of up to US$100,000, as demanded under *Shari'a*. A third demand was that daughters and sisters of Christian householders submit to marriage to militia chiefs. An Islamic cleric declared a *fatwa* that all Christian homes were now the rightful property of Muslims. Crosses were removed from churches. While some Sisters were out of their convent on business, they returned to find their home occupied by Islamist militia who were now turning it into a military headquarters. Elsewhere churches were converted into mosques.

With the evictions intensifying, not just in al-Dora, but also in Mosul and Kirkuk, Chaldean Auxiliary Bishop Shlemon Warduni of Baghdad told ACN: "Many families are obliged to leave their homes without being able to take anything with them. They are told they either have to be Muslim, or pay the *Jizya* – otherwise they will be killed." Speaking from Baghdad, he added: "People in the West do not believe in hell. They should come over here – they would soon change their minds. It is hell on earth here." Church leaders began tracking down Christian families most at risk and arranging for them to be given sanctuary in northern Iraq. Redemptorist priest Father Bashar Warda said: "If things go on like this, there will soon be hardly any Christians left in Baghdad."[103]

June 2007: ACN President Hans-Peter Rothlin appealed for prayer for Christians in Iraq, saying the Iraqi Church was "now in jeopardy" and adding: "The crisis facing the country's Christians is being totally ignored. By the time we realise what is going on, will it be too late?"

June 2007: Father Ragheed Aziz Ganni, 34, was gunned down close to the Holy Spirit parish church, Mosul, where he had just said Mass. Also killed with him were three deacons: Basman Yousef Daoud, Ghasan Bidawid and Wadid Hanna. After the killing on 3rd June, the priest received tributes from all over the world.

June 2007: A convent of Chaldean Sacred Heart nuns, in al-Dora, now an Islamic stronghold, was attacked by a group of terrorists. They seized their opportunity while some Sisters were away. When they returned, the Sisters found the convent looted and transformed into a military HQ.[104] That same day, two churches were attacked in the same part of Baghdad, the churches of Saint John the Baptist and Saint James. Reports suggest one of the churches was transformed into a mosque.[105]

June 2007: Father Hanni Abdel Ahad, in his 30s, was seized from the Church of Divine Widsom in the Suleikh district of north-east Baghdad.[106]

June 2007: Iraqi Christian leaders in the UK sent a letter to British Prime Minister Tony Blair, calling on him to devote his last days in office to saving Christianity in Iraq. The letter continues: "At this rate there will be no Christians at all in Baghdad, Mosul or Basra a decade from now."[107]

July 2007: Chaldean Auxiliary Bishop Andreas Abouna of Baghdad reported that Church leaders in the city had set up a mission centre for Christians forced from their homes by the wave of extremism. Up to 6,000 Christians were benefiting from the scheme which he said enabled them to feel safe. Bishop Abouna said: "It is not easy for our people; they are in need of everything." The bishop said that all churches in al-Dora were now closed and that the persecution had spread to Baghdad's Karkh region.[108]

October 2007: On a visit to London, Bishop Antoine Audo of Aleppo gave a speech saying: "This may be the end of Christianity in Iraq. It would be sad and dangerous for the Church, for Iraq and even for Muslims themselves, because it would mean the end of an old experience of living together. If Christians and Muslims are not able to exist in the Middle East, it will spell danger for the West in the future." He was speaking at an event hosted by the UK charity *Iraqi Christians in Need*.

October 2007: Father Pius Affas and Father Mazen Ishoa were kidnapped while travelling by car en route to Our Lady of Fatima's Church in Mosul's al-Faisaliya district. Bishop Abouna praised the priests' "outstanding witness" to the Church in times of persecution.

January 2008: Co-ordinated bomb-blasts targeted at least six church buildings in Mosul and Baghdad. Only one person was injured and the buildings suffered only minor damage with bombs placed some distance away from the churches. Church leaders were alarmed by the attacks' timing, which fell on Christmas Eve in many Orthodox communities and Epiphany for Catholics. Sources close to ACN who cannot be named for security reasons, said that *Sunni* and *Shi'a* Muslim extremists wanted to expel Christians from their respective areas of control.[109]

January 2008: Car bombers targeted two churches in Kirkuk – the cathedral, in the city centre, and the nearby St Afrem's Syrian Orthodox Church in the Al-Ummal residential district. Nobody was hurt.[110]

February 2008: Archbishop Louis Sako of Kirkuk announced plans for a 30-member Christian Council to represent the views of Christians in the city. The plans received support from President Talabani of Iraq on a visit to the region. Made up of five groups – Chaldeans, Armenians, Assyrians, Syrian Orthodox and Syrian-Catholics, the council's task is to examine social, cultural and inter-faith relations. Archbishop Sako told ACN: "For too long, the Christians have struggled to get their views heard in the main debates of the day because so often they do not speak with one voice."[111]

February 2008: Attackers kidnapped Archbishop Paulos Faraj Rahho of Mosul outside his cathedral. They killed his two bodyguards and a driver. The archbishop, who had just completed saying the Way of the Cross, was bundled into a car and driven off into captivity. After the incident on 29th February, fears grew for the archbishop's safety and health. The 65-year-old was reliant on daily medication for a heart complaint. His kidnappers demanded a ransom of up to US$3 million.

Nearly two weeks after the archbishop's capture, news came that he was dead. The kidnappers gave directions to a shallow grave site close to the centre of Mosul. En route to the funeral, Archbishop Sako told ACN in an interview: "Archbishop Rahho was a man who gave his life for his Church and for his people. Things for us have been getting worse and worse. Holy Week for us has come early and today is our Good Friday – we are living out Christ's passion spiritually and at all levels." Some weeks later, demonstrations were held protesting against alleged police inaction to hunt down his kidnappers.[112]

April 2008: Syrian Orthodox priest Father Youssef Adel Abody, aged 40, was shot dead in the district of Zayiuna, a Christian neighbourhood in Baghdad. The priest was reportedly travelling in his car when armed men opened fire. The priest was director of a high school attended by both Christians and Muslims. He had been the target of threats and intimidation intended to drive him away. Undaunted, he held a prayer meeting for all Christians. The funeral, in Baghdad's Karrada neighbourhood, was celebrated by the Syrian Orthodox Archbishop of Baghdad. Amid reports of continuing Christian emigration from Iraq, mourners at the funeral stated their determination to stay. "It is a question of faith," one said.[113]

July 2008: ACN reports from Mosul revealed that the number of displaced Iraqi Christians fleeing north, especially to the Nineveh plains outside Mosul, had shot up dramatically to 50,000. The source said that much of the exodus had taken place within the previous two years. He added that the mass emigration reflected growing alarm and despondency about the prospects for Christians in modern Iraq. The news raised further questions about the survival of Christianity in key parts of the country.

Profile: A tribute to Father Ragheed Ganni of Iraq (1972-2007)

Leaving church after Mass one Sunday, Father Ragheed Ganni was stopped in the road by armed men. One of them screamed at him: "I told you to close the church. Why didn't you do it? Why are you still here?" Father Ragheed Ganni replied: "How can I close the house of God?" His attackers pushed him to the ground before killing him and also the three sub-deacons with him at the time: Basman Yousef Daoud, Ghasan Bidawid and Wadid Hanna. Recalling the incident, Bayan Adam Bella, wife of Wahid Hanna, and the sole survivor of the incident, described how moments before his death, Father Ragheed had made a gesture to her with his head, urging her to run away. Speaking publicly for the first time a year after the murders on 3rd June 2007, Bayan said that Father Ragheed had a chance to escape when he caught sight of the attackers advancing. "He could have fled but he did not want to because he knew they were looking for him."[114]

Born on 20th January 1972, Ragheed Ganni grew up in northern Iraq, graduating in engineering from Mosul University in 1993. Sent to Rome, he gained a licentiate in ecumenical theology and in 2001 was ordained priest for the Chaldean Archdiocese of Mosul. Instead of returning to his native country, he stayed in Rome for a further two years to complete his studies. By the late summer of 2004, life in Iraq was becoming difficult for Christians with attacks on churches and suicide bombs. Among the places worst affected was Mosul but Father Ragheed insisted on going back. "That is where I belong," he said.[115] He said: "Saddam has fallen, we have elected a government, we have voted for a constitution."[116] He held theology courses for lay faithful, worked with the young, consoled disadvantaged families and was, at about the time of his death, helping a child with sight problems to receive treatment in Rome.

But the situation was getting worse all the time. After an attack on his parish on Palm Sunday (1st April 2007), he commented: "We empathise with Christ who entered Jerusalem in full knowledge that the consequences of his love for mankind was the cross. Thus, while bullets smashed our church windows, we offered up our suffering as a sign of love for God."

His spirit remained unbowed. Just a few weeks before his death, he wrote: "Each day we wait for the decisive attack but we will not stop celebrating Mass; we will do it underground where we are safer. I am encouraged in this decision by my parishioners. This is war, real now, but we hope to carry our cross to the very end with the help of Divine Grace."[117]

By this stage, the bombings and kidnappings were multiplying. Muslim extremists began to demand taxes from Christians to remain in their homes. Water and electricity became scarce. Father Ragheed grew tired. In his last email to *AsiaNews* on 28th May 2007, he admitted: "We are on the verge of collapse." He described how a bomb had exploded inside his church the day before – Pentecost Sunday. He wrote that seven car bombs had exploded plus a further 10 explosions – all in quick succession. A three-day curfew had been imposed. "We are prisoners in our own homes," he wrote. He pondered on the emergence of an increasingly 'sectarian' Iraq. For him it prompted the question: "Will there be any space for Christians? We have no support, no group who fights our cause." But then he rallied, adding: "I am certain about one thing: that the Holy Spirit will enlighten people so that they may work for the good of humanity in this world so full of evil."

After Father Ragheed was killed on 3rd June 2007, there were many tributes. One of them was from project staff at *Aid to the Church in Need*, which had helped fund his training in Rome. A particularly poignant message was one from Adnam Mokrani, a professor in Islamic studies at the Angelicum University. He had become a close friend of Father Ragheed while he was in Rome. Professor Mokrani wrote: "You [Father Ragheed] not only shared the suffering of your people but also joined your blood to the thousands of Iraqis killed each day. I will never forget the day of your ordination… with tears in your eyes you told me: 'Today, I have died to self.' I didn't understand it right away…but today, through your martyrdom I have understood that phrase. You have died…so that Christ would be raised up in you despite the sufferings, sorrows, despite the chaos and despite the madness."[118]

Israel and Palestine

	Israel	Palestine
Population	7 million	4 million
Major religions	Judaism Islam	Islam
Christian population	1.5% (160,000)	

World religious leaders have called on Churches in the West to help Christians in the Holy Land who are threatened by religious intolerance and deepening poverty. Emigration is such a serious problem that if it continues at current levels Christians will all but disappear. According to some senior clergy, Christians now make up more than 20 percent of emigrants. It is an alarming statistic given that Christians number about 160,000.

In 2008, the year that the state of Israel celebrated its 60th anniversary, reports showed that in the years the foundation of the state, Christians in Bethlehem declined from 60 percent to 10 percent of the population. In Jerusalem, the situation is just as serious. There, Christians have fallen from 45 percent of the population to barely 7,000 in number. Abandoning the Holy Land is for many a very painful decision. They know that the more people leave, the worse it becomes for those left behind.

The challenges are increased by the seemingly intractable political debate over the future of Israel and Palestine and the possible creation of a permanent Palestinian state. In Israel and the Occupied Territories, Islamic extremists have stepped up attacks on Christians who are often falsely branded as being pro-US

When in June 2007 Hamas, a militant Islamist group, seized power in Gaza, the problem of extremism suddenly intensified, sparking more attacks on minorities, not least Christians. But the concerns about extremism and intolerance were not confined to Gaza – they have affected the West Bank as well.

For many, especially Christians, the problems were compounded by Israel's continuing work on the so-called security barrier around the West Bank. For Christians in the Bethlehem area reliant on tourism, the increased security controls have deterred visitors, damaging the local economy. After 2007, however, there were signs of improvement.

Meanwhile, in Israel, Christians have suffered discrimination, as most are Arabs, which means they are not fully recognised as citizens. Reports show repeated government ambivalence in response to acts of discrimination against minority groups, especially Christians. Israeli police have been accused of inaction against attacks on Christians carried out by Druze, who are members of a religion derived from Islam.

January 2007: European and North American bishops declared that pilgrimages to the Holy Land were essential to the livelihood of the region's Christians. The bishops said they were also an important sign of solidarity to a suffering people. In a statement at the end of a visit to the region, the Coordination of Episcopal Conferences in support of Christians in the Holy Land spoke of the "moderating influence" of Christians which they said was "essential to achieving peace". It followed a trip the previous month by Anglican Archbishop Rowan Williams of Canterbury and Cardinal Cormac Murphy-O'Connor, Archbishop of Westminster, who both warned of the dangers of an emigrating Christian community. Dr Williams warned that if the exodus did not to stop "it would be a very bad signal for the Middle East and the rest of the world."[119]

March 2007: Patriarch-elect Fouad Twal of Jerusalem spoke out against the security barrier separating Israel from the West Bank: "The creation of a separating wall by the Israeli government, in particular inside and around Jerusalem, has heavily restricted access to mosques, churches and other holy places. It is a serious obstacle to the work of religious communities providing education, health services and other social humanitarian aid to the Palestinians. The separating wall has created problems for Christians in the Bethlehem area when they wish to visit the Basilica of the Holy Sepulchre in Jerusalem. It has made things far more complicated for Palestinian Christians living on the Israeli side of the wall visiting Christian sites in Bethany and Bethlehem. The wall and police cordons have also rendered impossible the clergy's movements to churches and monasteries in the West Bank... For many young people, Jerusalem is almost a myth, a city they have never seen, that belongs to the Biblical world."[120]

June 2007: Shortly after Hamas, the Islamist political movement, took power in Gaza, masked men from the party's military wing, *Ezzedine El Qassam*, attacked and looted the Latin Catholic Church in Gaza and a

59

nearby school run by the Nuns of the Rosary. According to Father Moussalem, the parish priest, the attackers ransacked the site. "They broke a number of crucifixes. They also set fire to the nuns' home, but thanks be to God, they were not present at that time. They stole computers, destroyed the photocopying machine and turned the place upside down."[121] Hanadi Missak, headteacher of the School of the Rosary, said: "At times the nuns are insulted or spat at when they are in the streets."[122]

September 2007: Addressing *Aid to the Church in Need*'s conference at Westminster Cathedral, London, Greek Catholic Archbishop Elias Chacour of Galilee described Christian emigration from the Holy Land as the Church's "biggest enemy". He said: "Christians need to impose their presence [in the Holy Land]. We need to say: 'We are here to stay'." Archbishop Chacour said that Christians made up more than 20 percent of emigrants from the Holy Land and yet they represented barely 1.5 percent of the population. He said: "We are seriously threatened by the possibility of disappearing."

October 2007: Rami Ayyad, the owner of Gaza's only Christian bookshop, was kidnapped and then shot. His body also showed traces of knife wounds and torture. Two years earlier, the victim – who was of Orthodox origin – joined the Evangelical Baptist Church. He worked for the Society of the Holy Bible, an international Baptist association. Six months before his death, his bookshop was set ablaze by a group called the Virtuous Swords of Islam. The group denounced his "Christian proselytism".[123]
In February 2008, four months after Mr Avyad's death, his wife, Pauline Avyad, gave birth in Gaza City to a baby girl. In an interview, Mrs Avyad said that police had made little progress investigating her husband's death. A Bible Society staff member reported that Christians "feel real pressures now between the Muslims and Christians in Gaza. Many of the Muslims believe that Rami was evangelising people; so it was OK to kill him."

December 2007: Allegations against Israel were made in relation to the appointment of Theophilus III, elected in August 2005 as the Patriarch of the Greek Orthodox Church in Jerusalem. Israel's support for the nomination, required in a tradition dating back to the era of the Ottoman Empire (1299-1923) and going on to the present day, continued to be denied for more than two years. Theophilus III responded by accusing Israel of putting pressure on him to approve controversial property transactions made by his predecessor, Ireneus I. Before he died, Ireneus was criticised for agreeing to sell property belonging to the patriarchate to Israeli property developers wanting to increase the amount of land in Jewish hands. The properties included hotels and shops near the Jaffa Gate, in Jerusalem's Old City. "I am not prepared to serve the specific interests of private businessmen to obtain the acknowledgement [by Israel of my appointment]," said Theophilus III.[124] Israel eventually acknowledged the new patriarch's appointment in December 2007 after interventions from the international community, including the Ecumenical Council of Churches.

December 2007: The leaders of Catholic charity *Aid to the Church in Need* expressed their shock after witnessing what ACN described as "the dangers threatening the survival of Christianity in the Holy Land". Following a week-long visit to Israel and Palestine to mark the 60th anniversary of the charity, the ACN delegation concluded that the Church's crucial role as a mediator between Muslim and Jewish communities "was being severely undermined by religious extremism, worsening poverty and emigration". The ACN group accused the West of making the problem worse by not speaking up on behalf of the suffering Christians.

In a statement afterwards, Hans-Peter Röthlin, ACN President and Father Joaquin Alliende, the International Ecclesiastical Assistant, wrote: "We learned again and again that the presence of Christians is now in jeopardy. It is a cause of much sorrow..." Mr Rothlin added: "We call upon Christians all over the world to pray – to pray that the hearts of the people will be changed. The Christians in Jerusalem, Bethlehem and Galilee are the descendants of the first followers of Christ. The ancient stones shouldn't just be seen as places to visit, like a museum, but they should be linked to the living stones, the faithful of Christ."[125]

May 2008: One night, armed attackers broke into a Christian school in Gaza City's Zaitoon Quarter, beating and tying up two security guards and stealing a bus belonging to the Palestinian Bible Society. The reports from the Palestinian Centre for Human Rights went on to stress the increasing fear and instability of Christians in the Gaza Strip. They made special mention of the murder of Gaza Bible bookshop owner Rami Ayyad and the bomb outside the Zawha Rosary School, run by nuns.[126]

Kazakhstan

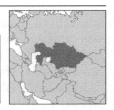

Population	Religions	Christian Population
15.4 million	Muslim 47% Orthodox 44% Protestant 2% Other 7%	7.5 million

Kazakhstan's draft Religion Law, presented to parliament for its first reading on 11th June 2008, introduces harsher penalties for unregistered religious activity. Local religious groups would be banned from carrying out educational, publishing and missionary work.[127] Numbers of foreign missionaries would be strictly controlled and unregistered ones would be expelled. The law also tightens up planning regulations, which may lead to church buildings being forced to close. Archbishop Jan Lenga of Karaganda said the law would take the Church back to the oppression and controls of Stalinist times. The proposed legislation could force more than 70 of Kazakhstan's Catholic priests to stop ministering in the country, leaving only seven active. The archbishop added: "This proposed law is against all non-Orthodox and will hit us." Parliament has set a deadline of 1st December 2008 for the law to be adopted.[128]

The new law comes despite several government promises about tolerance and respect for religious freedom. Reports say that driving such statements is the government's dream of chairing the Organisation for Security and Cooperation in Europe (OSCE) in 2010.[129] At an OSCE conference Amanbek Mukhashev, deputy head of the Religious Affairs Committee, said: "Today we can declare with complete assurance that in Kazakhstan all the necessary conditions have been created for the full freedom of thought, conscience, religion and belief."[130]

Religious minorities who are unregistered – either by choice or because of difficulties applying – are exposed to various forms of persecution, in particular heavy economic sanctions. This follows draconian changes to the 1992 law on freedom of conscience, especially the 2005 amendments on "national security" and measures concerning the "fight against terrorism". As a result, missionary activity has been curbed and unregistered groups have been effectively outlawed. Protestant groups belonging to the Council of Baptist Churches face the greatest difficulties, since they refuse on principle to apply for registration. Registration can involve granting the state the right to interfere in internal affairs. Officials can request personal information such as members' ethnic origin, profession, political preferences, and the names of the pastor's personal friends.[131] Recently, many Baptist clergymen have been fined under the laws prohibiting religious activities by unregistered groups. In March 2008, Pyotr Panafidin and Ivan Friesen were each fined the equivalent of US$970 – a sum equal to three months' salary for the average worker.[132] Failure to pay may lead to property being impounded or wages being docked.

Despite growing problems, there have been some positive developments. For the first time in the country's history, two religious festivities have been introduced into the Kazakh calendar: Christmas, according to the Orthodox dating, and *Eid al-Adha*, the Muslim feast of sacrifice.[133]

September 2007: Four members of the Grace Presbyterian Church – including its leader, Igor Kim – were investigated on charges of treason by the KNB (National Security Committee). 12 church members began a hunger strike to protest against the investigations.[134]

January 2008: The KNB carried out a 17-hour raid on the Grace Presbyterian Church in the city of Almaty, confiscating all the church's computer hardware.[135]

January-February 2008: Within a two-month period, 14 Protestant churches in Almaty were subjected to heavy-handed safety and security checks. The Protestant Alpha and Omega Centre faced a two-day investigation after it received harsh criticism on television.[136]

March 2008: Government officials warned Baptist leader Dmitry Jantsen that his church and several others would be closed down and that he would be jailed. Justice Department minister Serik Tlekbaev told him not to try to appeal to international organisations such as the United Nations or the Organisation for Security and Cooperation in Europe (OSCE), because "they will not be of any help to you." Tlekbaev denies the claims.[137]

June 2008: An ACN fact-finding and project assessment trip to Kazakhstan revealed growing concerns over the proposed Religion Law. Archbishop Lenga described the law as "a disaster", saying "it is against all non-Orthodox and will hit us." But the bishops still hoped for a satisfactory resolution before the law is adopted.[138]

Lebanon

Population	Religions	Christian Population
4 million	Christian 54% Muslim 45% Other 1%	2 million

Lebanon is experiencing a period of serious tension as it makes the long road to recovery following the 2006 'July War' between Hezbollah, a *Shi'a* hard-line movement, and neighbouring Israel. The conflict left more than 1,000 people dead, mostly Lebanese civilians, and displaced up to one million people. The country's infrastructure was also severely crippled.

Article 9 of the constitution establishes respect for all religions and guarantees them autonomy on issues such as marriage and inheritance. The balance of power in Lebanon shows how religious differences are never far beneath the surface. The president of the republic is always a Maronite Catholic, the presidency of the Council of Ministers is the preserve of a *Sunni* Muslim and the parliamentary Speaker has to be a *Shi'a* Muslim. Religious communities are also represented in parliament according to fixed quotas. But despite the tensions, Lebanon has long held a reputation as being the best in the Middle East for religious freedom. Religious groups are permitted to organise their own schools, associations and religious courts.

However, Christians experience latent persecution, and the Islamization of society poses a threat to them. In the Chouf region, where more than 50 percent of the population are Christians, there are no Christian employees in government. In July 2007, Maronite Bishop Béchara Rai of Byblos spoke out against the "Islamization schemes" for Lebanon. Bishop Rai also accused the government of behaving as though Lebanon was "a theocratic Islamic State", in choosing to sign the "Charter of children's rights in Islam" (Decree 636). He said: "With this decree, the government is ignoring the presence of the Christians and infringing Article 9 of the constitution, the coexistence pact and the particular and specific character of Lebanon, transforming it into an Islamic state and society." Bishop Rai asked the government to withdraw the decree – later presented to Parliament as a draft bill – and thereby safeguard religious liberty in the country.[139]

Thousands of Iraqi refugees arriving in Lebanon have been refused temporary legal status by the authorities. The refugees, many of them Christians, are therefore left with only two choices: prison or returning to Iraq. Bishop Michel Kassarji of Beirut reported that he was caring for 800 families (up to 5,000 people), almost all of whom were illegal immigrants. Lebanon has Palestinian refugee camps dating from the 1948 conflict, but has never signed the 1951 International Convention on Refugees. As a result, the government refuses access to foreign refugees other than those granted a temporary permit by the UN en route to another country.

January 2007: Hackers broke into the website of the International Catholic Union for the Press (UCIP) in Lebanon. The contents were deleted and replaced by material in Arabic. This was the second attack recorded on a Christian website in the space of two weeks. On 13th January, the website of the Council of Middle Eastern Churches was deleted and replaced entirely with extremist Islamic propaganda material. The Arab press attributed this attack to unidentified "non-Christian extremist movements". Father Tony Khadra, director of UCIP's Beirut offices, spoke of "an attack on the shared values of coexistence between Christianity and Islam". The priest said the underlying reason for the attack was that both websites were committed to reporting on initiatives promoting dialogue between Muslims and Christians.

April 2007: Government authorities cancelled the holiday on Good Friday, without discussing the matter with religious authorities.[140]

Maldives

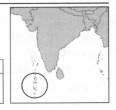

Population	Religions	Christian Population
306,000	Muslim 99%	Unknown[141]
	Other 1%	

President Maumoon Abdul Gayoom of the Maldives declared in July 2000 that the country was exclusively Islamic. He went on to accuse foreigners of seeking to destroy the religious unity of the people by introducing other faiths.[142] Referring to the country's official adoption of Islam in 1153, an official government statement read: "Being a 100 percent Muslim country, the national religion is Islam. Islam is the religion of the state and the backbone of the society."[143] The declaration reflects Article 7 of the country's 1998 constitution, which defines Islam as the state religion, and restricts all political, judicial and administrative positions to Muslims.

In this nation made up of more than 1,000 islands, the government enforces *Shari'a* law and has banned non-Muslims from expressing their faith in public. Conversion from Islam is outlawed and building churches is strictly prohibited. It is a far cry from the 19th century when the Maldives was under British control; the colonial power presented the government with a local language edition of the Bible. The fate of this project remains unknown although it is likely the book was either destroyed or hidden. Until the 1980s, there were no known Christians but since the 1970s, the secret distribution of Church literature has led to some illicit conversions.

To avoid detection, Christians are forced to practise their faith in secret and hence their total number is unknown. They face the threat of 're-conversion' back to Islam or loss of citizenship. Foreign tourists are permitted to practise their faith in private, providing no locals are present during their religious activities. Importing Bibles or any Christian literature is strictly forbidden. Tourists are however permitted to bring single copies for personal use. Although Christian rights' organisations such as *Open Doors* did not receive any reports about arrests of indigenous believers during 2007, the Maldives continued to cause concern. Hence, the country remained on *Open Doors*' top 10 list of countries where Christians are persecuted the most.[144]

September 2007: About 12 foreign tourists were injured when a bomb exploded in Sultan Male Park, a major landmark. The explosion was blamed on Islamic extremists who are accused of trying to stop foreign tourists from visiting the Maldives. The fundamentalists claim the tourists promote a culture "contrary" to Islam. But the local population wants to preserve the lucrative tourist industry. President Gayoom issued a decree banning foreign imams from entering the country; similarly, he has prohibited women from wearing the *hijab* and other clothes which cover the whole body. The President has also declared that foreign *madrassas* (Islamic schools) and seminaries cannot be recognised as educational institutions. In early October police raided an island about 70 miles south of the Maldives' capital, Malé, which is considered to be a stronghold of Islamic extremism. Clashes were reported and police arrested 50 people.

November 2007: Special Majlis (the constitutional assembly) passed an amendment which would restrict Maldivian citizenship to Muslims.

May 2008: The country's Information Minister, Mohamed Nasheed, stated on his personal blog that Maldivians who convert away from Islam, or who are the children of Maldivians married to non-Muslims, may be at risk of losing their citizenship under a new draft constitution. The attorney general's office has highlighted more than 200 issues of consistency, wording and practicality, which need to be addressed by the constitutional drafting committee and Special Majlis before the constitution can be ratified. However, his list of problem areas does not include the question of citizenship.[145] Ironically these changes to the constitution were initiated by President Gayoom as part of The Democratic Reform Agenda which has the expressed the intention of "strengthening democracy and enhancing human rights protection".[146]

Nigeria

Population	Religions	Christian Population
148 million	Muslim 50% Christian 40% Animist 10%	59 million

Victory for Umaru Yar'Adua in the April 2007 presidential elections could prove crucial in determining the outcome of Nigeria's long-running religious tensions. A Muslim, Yar'Adua was governor of Kastrina when the state adopted *Shari'a* Islamic law back in 2000, one of 12 to do so. But Yar'Adua insisted at the time that non-Muslims in his state would be guaranteed security and independence. Now, many expect him to uphold the rights of Christians as well as Muslims, noting how his bid for the presidency was backed by the then incumbent, Olusegun Obasanjo, a leading Christian. As President, Yar'Adua has pledged to uphold his predecessor's commitment to social and religious cohesion.

But for Nigeria's large Christian population, religious freedom in a *Shari'a* system is hugely problematic and as yet there is no sign that the tensions of the past will disappear. In principle *Shari'a* law does not apply to non-Muslims in civil and criminal matters. And yet, the lives of many non-Muslims in Nigeria have been affected in various ways. In Kano State public consumption and distribution of alcohol is banned; in other states alcohol can only be consumed inside federal buildings like police stations.

One priest told *Aid to the Church in Need* that indigenous people from Kano who refuse to abandon their Christian names risk losing rights and privileges. According to sources in Yobe state, a Christian name alone bars an applicant from a government post, In Zamfara State many public facilities are strictly segregated by sex. Meantime, in Maiduguri, Borno State, a source close to ACN spoke of a ban on Christian public rallies and outdoor services. The source said indigenous people in the region who had converted to Christianity risked being killed by extremists.

Christian communities in the 12 *Shari'a* states have experienced widespread religious intolerance and discrimination. These include Christian students and teachers facing trumped up charges for blaspheming against Islam, a court action which forced them to leave school. Elsewhere, Christians are repeatedly denied permits to build churches and cemeteries.

Church buildings are destroyed after being judged illegal. Christian teenagers are abducted and forced to convert, especially girls given in marriage to Muslim men. And Muslims who convert to Christianity are intimidated and receive death threats. In some cases, Christians are forced to go before *Shari'a* courts, even though they have the right not be judged by such tribunals.[147] Other reports describe how Christian girls are compelled to wear Islamic dress in public schools.[148]

But work to ease inter-religious tension continues. Inter-faith dialogue is strong thanks to initiatives by non-governmental organisations such as Kano's Inter-Ethnic Forum and Kaduna's Inter-Faith Mediation Centre and Muslim/Christian Dialogue Forum. In Kano and Kaduna, sectarian violence has broken out periodically and was particularly bad in 2004. In June 2007 incoming President Umaru Yar'Adua pledged to set up an Advisory Inter-Faith Council to prevent inter-communal violence.

One case illustrates the extreme situation some Christians face. In December 2006, a 15-year-old Muslim named Farida converted to Christianity. Her husband immediately divorced her. Returning to her family home, she was told to revert to Islam. Matters came to a head when Farida's mother asked her to boil some water. The mother then asked her to choose between Islam and being scalded with water. When Farida refused to convert, her mother poured the boiling water on her. Farida's upper torso was seriously injured and she had third degree burns on her arm. Taken into hiding by the Church, she has since given birth to a baby girl.[149]

January 2007: A high school chapel in Wusasa, Kaduna state, was set ablaze for the third time. In the latest incident, the chapel was attacked by Muslim students. It had been set upon only a month previously. On both occasions, the building was saved thanks to staff and students at the school. The building had only been rebuilt five months previously. Before the most recent arson attempt, letters were left in the chapel warning of an attack unless staff and students left the school.[150]

March 2007: An Evangelical teacher in Gombe state was accused of desecrating a copy of the *Qur'an*. She was beaten and killed, and her body was burnt at a high school in the town of Gandu. Two days later a church was set ablaze in the same town. 16 people arrested for the teacher's murder were later released. Later, her attackers were heard chanting the names of other Christian teachers. The teachers began a strike calling for better police protection and justice for the murder of their colleague.[151]

March 2007: A Christian boy kidnapped in November 2006 escaped and returned to his family home. Resisting calls to convert, 13-year-old Victor Udo Usen fled to a shop run by his mother in Sokoto state. His parents arranged for him to be evacuated from the city.[152]

June 2007: Pastor Adamu Sunday Peni, from Kebbi State, spoke out against the exclusion of Christians from state government posts. In the entire state public service there is only one non-Muslim top official.[153]

September 2007: Nearly 20 Christians were killed, more than 60 people were injured and a further 500 were displaced when Muslim youths in Kano State went on the rampage. They torched nine churches and attacked businesses and homes owned by non-Muslims. The violence began at a school when Christian students (of whom there are 14 out of a student body of 1,500) were accused of drawing a picture of the prophet Mohammed on a mosque wall.[154]

October 2007: Two young Christian men were murdered during Ramadan after a sheikh urged Muslims in the city of Kaduna (Kaduna State), to wage *jihad* against infidels during a broadcast on state television.[155]

November 2007: Muslims attacked Christians in Gani town and in a nearby Christian settlement, destroying their houses and shops, injuring several people and killing school teacher Danyaro Bala. The violence started when the media reported that a Christian candidate was ahead in the polls.[156]

November 2007: Kano state government unilaterally decided to demolish four churches to make way for roads and a hospital. Two Pentecostal churches and two churches belonging to the Evangelical Church of West Africa (ECWA) were due for demolition under the government's plan. There was no discussion beforehand and no offer of compensation.[157]

November 2007: A report investigating the killings of Christians at a school in Tudun Wada Dankadai, Kano state, stated that only three had died and claimed that fellow Christians were responsible. However, it was widely thought that as many as 19 Christians had died and that the riots had been started by Muslim students and an Islamic preacher. Later it was claimed that the nine Muslims on the committee which produced the report had over-ruled their three Christian counterparts. The committee's report maintained that only three deaths could be confirmed because the other 16 could not be officially identified, as they were buried in a common grave.[158]

December 2007: Ten people were killed and three churches were set on fire in Bauchi state after Muslims discovered that two foundation stones had been removed from a mosque under construction. Dozens of Christians' homes were attacked. A teacher at Baba Tanko Secondary School said Muslim students began attacking Christians in their classes: "They also attacked their Christian colleagues with knives and daggers. I had to run for my dear life because the situation became uncontrollable."[159]

February 2008: A policeman was killed and two Christian teenagers were injured in Sumaila (Kano state). It happened when Muslim high school students rioted over claims that a Christian student wrote a "blasphemous" article on the prophet Mohammed. After injuring the Christian students, the mob went to the town's police station, where they killed a Christian police officer, Inspector Jibrin Garba, and burned down the station. Ahmadu Inuwa, a student who suffered knife and machete wounds, said the accused Christian student, Ashiru Danlami, could not have written the English language article as he could hardly speak English, much less write it.[160]

February 2008: A rampage in Yana (Bauchi State) that left one Christian dead, seven others hospitalised and destroyed five churches, took place after a Christian woman refused a Muslim man's offer of marriage. The Muslim man gathered friends and neighbours that night to tell them that the woman, Patience Yusuf, had blasphemed against Mohammed.[161]

February 2008: Father David Helon reported that in Yala town (Bauchi State), four Protestant churches were burnt and that the interior fittings of a Catholic church (altar cloths, pews and sacred images) were ripped out and destroyed. He said in Bauchi, Churches are often not compensated for buildings damaged during religious riots.[162]

March 2008: Kano state authorities once again refused plans to build a church 28 years after the project was first conceived. Over the course of 15 months, the temporary church they have used was torched three times. Excrement has been founded smeared on its walls. On Christmas Eve 2006, the building's thatched roof was set alight.[163]

North Korea

Population	Religions	Christian Pop.
2 million	Agnostic/Atheist: 71% New religions 13% Animist 12.5% Christian 2%, Other 1.5%	500,000

The communist regime of Kim Jong-Il claims that the country enjoys religious freedom but in reality the situation is very different. Religious liberty is enshrined in the constitution, but the communist government requires the faithful to join party-controlled organisations, such as the North Korean Catholic Association. According to official government figures there are 10,000 Buddhists, 10,000 Protestants and 4,000 Catholics, but these estimates refer only to members of officially sanctioned associations. Anyone practising religion outside an approved association has fewer opportunities for education, employment and food assistance.

In the capital, Pyongyang, there are four churches, two Protestant, one Catholic, and one Orthodox. A 2004 report by *Aid to the Church in Need* (Italy) described the two Protestant churches as mouthpieces for the regime's propaganda. Their pastors are said to liken Kim Jong-Il to a god. In the only Catholic church, there is no North Korean priest, but community prayers are held once a week. In exceptional cases, religious functions are led by ethnic Korean priests, of foreign nationality. Following the inauguration of a new Orthodox church in August 2007, Catholics are the only community without a priest.

Since the communist regime was established in 1953 about 300,000 Christians have disappeared – they are assumed to be dead. Some 80,000 people are thought to be languishing in labour camps, subject to starvation and torture. No one can say whether these figures are accurate. They are provided by NGO officials in the country who wish to remain anonymous. Former North Korean officials and ex-prisoners have said that Christians in re-education camps or prisons are treated worse than other detainees.

The Vatican highlights the persecution of Christians in North Korea by continuing to list in its annual directory of bishops the details of a Bishop of Pyongyang aged over 100 and who has not been seen since 1962. The 2008 edition of *Annuario Pontificio* refers to Monsignor Francis Hong Yong-ho, born in 1906 and consecrated bishop in 1944.[164]

72

However, there are signs of hope. Whereas Christian workers were once treated as Western spies, they are now welcomed. As part of this 'new attitude' taken by government, a medical facility in Hamgyeongbuk-do province was built with the assistance of the Catholic International Cooperation Medical Service. When in December 2007 the Korean bishops visited Rome for their *Ad Limina* meeting with the Pope, Benedict XVI said: "I am...aware of the practical gestures of reconciliation undertaken for the well-being of those in North Korea."

September 2007: A confidential document sent to military barracks around the country described religion "spreading like a cancer inside North Korea's armed forces, whose mission is to defend socialism. [It] must be eradicated without delay." The booklet warned: "They are placing spies within international delegations entering our borders to spread their religions and superstitious beliefs... [This material] is like poison that corrupts socialism and paralyses class consciousness". Soldiers are warned to be on the look out for it "now more than ever".[165]

April 2008: A report by the US Commission on International Religious Freedom said that North Koreans with Christian links were likely to suffer worse than others when expatriated from China to their country of origin. The report stated that border guards reserved the harshest punishment for those who admitted to having contact with Christians. People who had been repatriated, and were found guilty of breaking North Korea's rules on religion, risked torture and imprisonment "more than anyone else". One refugee said: "If you get caught carrying a Bible, there is no way to save your life." Tens of thousands of North Koreans are estimated to be in China illegally; many are used as free manual labour, under the threat of repatriation. The report called on the Chinese government to respect international treaties on the right to political asylum. However, Beijing defended its policy of repatriation, citing a 25-year-old treaty with Pyongyang that guarantees the return of those who leave North Korea without documentation.[166]

Pakistan

Population	Religions	Christian Population
164 million	Islam 95% Hindu 1.5% Christian 1.5% Other 2%	2.5 million

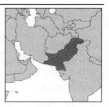

The assassination of Benazir Bhutto in December 2007 temporarily united the country in grief. Bishop Joseph Coutts described "unprecedented" levels of Cooperation between Christians and Muslims, with joint prayer services in her memory taking place across his diocese of Faisalabad. For many Christians, Bhutto and her Pakistan Peoples Party held out the promise of equal rights in a country where they are a beleaguered minority.

In the last few years, there has been a dramatic increase in the number of attacks against religious minorities across the country. Often these attacks have taken the form of *fatwas* (rulings by Islamic courts, sometimes calling for a person's death). They have also included attacks against churches and the abduction and attempted conversion of Christians.

The worst instrument of religious repression is the blasphemy law, which continues to claim many victims. This refers to sections B and C of Article 295 of Pakistan's Penal Code, whereby offences against the *Qur'an* are punishable by life imprisonment, and acts "defiling the sacred name of the Prophet Mohammed" are punishable with life imprisonment or death. There are also the *hudud* ordinances – *Qur'an*-inspired legal punishments that include flogging and stoning for activities such as adultery, gambling, and drinking alcohol.

According to the country's Catholic Justice and Peace Commission, the blasphemy law is "like the sword of Damocles hanging over Pakistani minorities, in addition to being a clear violation of their religious and human rights as guaranteed by the constitution". Khalil Tahir, head of the Adal Trust, which helps the Christian community to defend itself against false accusations, told *AsiaNews* that most of "those accused under the blasphemy law are from the social and religious minorities". Muslims have increasingly taken the law into their own hands in cases of alleged blasphemy. As a result, Christian churches, homes, hospitals and schools have been destroyed.

In May 2007, Archbishop Lawrence Saldanha of Lahore warned that extremist Muslims across the country were now trying to force Christians to convert by threatening violence. He spoke of growing calls for *Shari'a* Islamic law to be implemented. He said 500 Christians in north-west Pakistan had recently received anonymous letters warning them that they would be killed and their churches closed if they failed to become Muslims within 10 days. Archbishop Saldanha said: "It distresses us that Christians are threatened in an attempt to force them to convert to Islam. This is something that has never happened before."[167] The archbishop's comments come at a time of increasing anxiety over the future of Christianity in the country.

January 2007: Martha Bibi, a Christian woman from the village of Kot Nanak Singh (Kasur district), was charged under the blasphemy law and was held in custody for five months even though no evidence against her was given in court. Martha's problems began when she demanded payment for tools she rented to help build a mosque. When she visited the mosque construction site, she was refused payment. Undaunted, she began collecting up her tools and as she did so was beaten severely. She only escaped thanks to help from passers-by. That night the mosque's imam accused her of insulting the *Qur'an* and the prophet Mohammed and police charged her under the blasphemy law.

February 2007: Bishop Joseph Coutts of Faisalabad and two Muslims, a journalist and an academic, received death threats for taking part in an inter-faith meeting a few months earlier. An Islamist group called the Islamic Soldiers' Front claimed responsibility for the threatening letters and telephone calls in which all three men were branded as "infidels".

March 2007: In the Punjab province a Christian man was attacked by a mob of 150 Muslims who beat and tortured him for hours, accusing him of desecrating a copy of the *Qur'an*. The attack ended when the police moved in, but instead of arresting the aggressors they arrested the victim for allegedly violating the blasphemy law.

July 2007: Sadiq Masih, a 45-year-old Protestant, was mortally wounded in his own home by members of the Chaudri family, his former employers. He had quit his job at the family farm, tired of the endless abuse he received for being Christian.

August 2007: Arif Khan, 50, a Baptist bishop in Rawalpindi, and his wife Kathleen, 45, both US nationals, were murdered in nearby Islamabad. Two Christians from the city of Wana were arrested for the crime. However, according to local Christian sources, the actual perpetrator of the crime was a Muslim named Said Alam.

September 2007: Bo Brekke, 50, a Norwegian Christian heading a Salvation Army delegation, was murdered in his Lahore office. He had been in the country for a year.

October 2007: Three Christian children were refused entry into shelters in Rawalpindi. The children were then moved to a government shelter for women in Islamabad. The managers of the shelters were heavily criticised by NGO representatives.[168]

October 2007: Masked men kidnapped two Christians, Naeem Masih and Shahbaz Masih, in front of a hospital in North Waziristan. Nobody claimed responsibility for the kidnappings.[169]

December 2007: Hundreds of Christians staged a demonstration outside the Governor's House in Lahore to protest against the demolition of a church in Garden Town, Lahore. They begged for it to be rebuilt. Earlier, armed men forced their way into the church and ordered the minister and his family to leave and remove their belongings. Outside was a large deployment of police who held back a crowd of Christians who were determined to stop the destruction of the church.[170]

December 2007: A Christian doctor, Rejinald Humayun Zaheeruddin, medical superintendent at Pennell Memorial Christian Hospital, and his driver, were kidnapped by masked men in Bannu, North West Frontier Province. The doctor had served there for the past 25 years and treated patients of all religions, mainly Muslims.[171]

January 2008: Five Christians, Altaf Masih, Babar Masih, Emmanuel, Sakhawat Masih and Imran Masih were kidnapped at gunpoint near the Afghan border, and beaten on suspicion of selling alcohol. They were told to stop selling alcohol and were released a few days later.[172]

February 2008: Haroon, a young Catholic father of four, was kidnapped near Narang, 30 miles north of Lahore. He was ordered to telephone his wife and tell her that he would be killed if she dared to inform the police. He escaped after his captors left him unguarded one morning. By this stage, he had been moved to a number of different locations, finally ending up in a farmhouse 300 miles from Lahore.[173]

June 2008: Visiting Rome for their five-yearly *Ad Limina* meeting, Pakistan's Catholic bishops told Pope Benedict XVI that attitudes towards the Church had changed almost beyond recognition. Archbishop Lawrence Saldanha of Lahore, president of the Pakistan's Bishops' Conference, informed the Pontiff that while in the past the Church had been respected for its work in education and medicine, "today we carry out our mission in a hostile and conservative Islamic milieu that is increasingly extremist, intolerant and militant."[174]

June 2008: Two Christian girls – aged 13 and 10 – were kidnapped and were forced to convert to Islam and marry Muslim men. The Catholic Church's National Council for Justice and Peace said three men abducted Saba, 13 and 10-year-old Auila Younis in Muzaffargarh, Punjab Province. The NCJP has appealed to the Punjab's Chief Minister for the girls to be returned to their family. The local courts refused to intervene.[175]

July 2008: Bishop Max Rodrigues of Hyderabad said that despite a widespread shift towards a "theocratic" form of Islam, Christian communities had developed significant out-reach initiatives to non-Muslims. In an interview with ACN, the bishop said that he was using ACN's *Child's Bible* in evangelisation work among tribal peoples in the Sindh province of south-east Pakistan. He said there were now 17 catechists among the tribal community. He added: "The task of evangelisation in a theocratic country, strongly Islamicised… is a difficult thing but in my diocese there is a large tribal apostolate." The bishop said the pastoral work was revolutionising attitudes to women. He said: "The pastoral teams have changed the way that people think, and uplifted the status of women – women were seen as chattels, they had never sent girls to school as they didn't see the value in educating them, but now they send them to school as well."[176]

Profile: Sister Gladys Bashir

Principal, Fatima Convent School, Renala Khurd, Pakistan[177]

"If they want to kill me, then let them... They will kill me wherever I am."

To look at Sister Bashir, no one would ever guess that her story involves murder, tense stand-offs with local Muslim leaders, and accusations of blasphemy that could have resulted in her being imprisoned for life. Nor, given all that, would one imagine that she is a school headmistress.

Sister Bashir was appointed principal of Fatima Convent School, in Renala Khurd, Okara District in 2002. Like all Catholic schools, it was taken out of the Church's hands and nationalised by the Pakistani government in 1972. But 30 years later, following declining educational standards, the government gave the school back to the Church.

Former principal Shahzina Sadique opposed the move to return the school to the Church, and when the time for the handover came she made herself scarce so she would not have to go through with it. In her absence the board of governors decided to transfer control to the Franciscan Sisters. However, local *Mullahs* (Islamic leaders) arrived at the school to oppose the hand-over. Police had to be called to calm the situation and only then could a representative from the Board of Education go ahead with the transfer.

When Sister Gladys first entered the school buildings, she found that all the furniture had been taken – not so much as one chair was left. All the light bulbs had been taken out of their sockets and smashed. Students had to sit on the ground on bare boards, until one of the Sisters fetched an old carpet from the church for them to sit on. Later the Bishop of Faisalabad provided money for new furniture.

That was not all. The Sisters found that all the administrative papers were missing. They did not even know the names of the students at the school.

Initially children and parents were antagonistic towards the Sisters. Sister Galdys described it as "very discouraging for the teachers". Children even tried to physically abuse staff, attempting to push them over.

Shortly after the handover, Sister Gladys was yelled at by older students, who screamed: "This is not your school." But some of them had a change of heart. Later when she was in her office, one of the students who had been so vocal earlier came to seek reconciliation.

However, Shahzina Sadique, the old principal, had kept some of the keys and organised an occupation of the school buildings. During the lock in, the Sisters took a delegation, including Muslim teachers, to confront Ms Sadique. The occupation continued until 3am, when the Military and Police came and sealed the school. Sister Gladys was given the school keys by an official, and was provided with a police escort so that she could re-open the school safely later that day.

But Ms Sadique's campaign was not over and she accused Sister Gladys of burning the *Qur'an*. Under Pakistan's penal code: "Whoever wilfully defiles, damages or desecrates a copy of the Holy *Qur'an* or of an extract from it … shall be punishable with imprisonment for life." However, the Muslim teachers at the school backed up Sister Gladys, defending her innocence, and charges were eventually dropped.

By January, many of these difficulties had been settled, but that did not give much time to prepare for the public examinations at the end of March. Sister Gladys appealed for children to behave until they had sat the certificate, saying they needed to focus on their education and could leave after the exams if they wanted to. Some left, but new students replaced them. Both they and their parents were sympathetic to the school's ethos.

But in July the parish priest, Father George Ibrahim, who had been at the forefront of the campaign for the school, was killed. He had received death threats from former principal, Shahzina Sadique. Sometime after midnight on 4th July, 2003, armed men entered the church grounds and killed him. A post-mortem revealed that he died on the spot having been shot six times.

There was concern that Sisters would also be shot. Their white habit stands out from the colourful dress worn by most women in the region. Despite receiving death threats, Sister Gladys remained in Renala Khurd. She said: "If they want to kill me, then let them. If they want to kill me they will kill me wherever I am".

Sister Gladys is very tired after six years of fighting, but she says that there are no problems any more, and the school is getting very good results.

79

Russia

Population	Religions	Christian Population
142 million	Christian 57% Agnostic 33% Muslim 8% Other 2%	81 million

The dominant Russian Orthodox Church still shows signs of resistance to the presence of other Christian communities in Russia. However, its frosty attitude to the Catholic Church is beginning to thaw as circumstances bring the two Churches closer together. Indeed, since 2006, there have been distinct signs of improvement in Catholic–Russian Orthodox relations.

Key to this process has been the election of Benedict XVI as Pope. A world-renowned theologian, he is recognised for his awareness of contemporary issues and his respect for tradition. The Russian press, for example, reacted positively to his 2006 encyclical *Deus caritas est*.[178]

Following Benedict XVI's 2006 speech in Regensburg, Germany, the Orthodox Church expressed support for the Pontiff.[179] Hegumen Filaret (Bulekov), who represents the Russian Orthodox Church in Strasbourg, urged Muslims to be "more balanced [in their] reactions", declaring that the Pope's words had been misinterpreted and "politicised".[180] The Russian national press gave the story front page coverage, emphasising the Pontiff's viewpoint and the provocative nature of the criticism against him.[181]

Russia's respect for the Pope was confirmed on 13th March 2007 when President Vladimir Putin visited Benedict XVI in Rome. Barely a month later, an 81st birthday broadcast by the Pontiff on Russian state television was hailed as a landmark in Orthodox–Catholic relations. (See pp. 82-83 – Pope's 81st Birthday Broadcast to Russia)

The problem of religious education continued to be widely debated as disagreements raged over whether students should study religion in general or focus on Orthodoxy (or Islam in regions with a Muslim majority). The Orthodox Church campaigned for of a non-compulsory subject called 'Foundations of Orthodox culture' which is already running on an optional basis in some places, Meanwhile the Ministry for Education preferred a course called 'History of Religions'.

Pastor Andrei Karchev of the Kingdom of God Pentecostal Church objected to Orthodox Culture classes being run for a second year in schools in Belgorod, a city in western Russia. Although the subject is not compulsory, Pastor Karchev and other parents were unable to withdraw their children from the classes.[182] On 13th November 2007, Russia's lower house of parliament, the *Duma,* approved a number of amendments to the education Law. It abolished the 'Foundations of Orthodox culture' after 1st September 2009, in spite of formal protests by Russian Orthodox Patriarch Patriarch Aleksi II and the Holy Synod.[183]

July 2007: An open letter to President Putin appeared in the press, signed by 10 academics, including Nobel Prize winners Žorev Alferov and Vitalij Ginzburg, asking him to stop the "clericalization of society". They urged him against acknowledging theology as a subject for study and called for a ban on the 'Foundations of Orthodox culture' being taught in schools.[184]

August 2007: Police dispersed a protest organised by about 20 Orthodox believers in Puškin Square, Moscow, demanding that the Passion of Christ monastery be rebuilt. It was demolished in 1936-37. Three protesters who refused to leave were charged with holding an unauthorised protest.[185]

October 2007: Changes to the visa system were made, restricting the length of stay for foreigners entering Russia. Concerns were expressed about the likely impact on foreign priests and others working in the country.[186]

January 2008: In Samara region the Old Believers (who separated from the Russian Orthodox in 1666-67 over liturgical reforms) feared that building permission for their half-built church would be removed. They have been unable to recover churches confiscated in Soviet times, despite a 2003 presidential decree ordering their return.[187]

February 2008: At the request of Russian Orthodox Bishop Ignati of Vyazma, officials and police in Smolensk investigated a local Methodist church. Intimidated by the interference in their affairs, only five Methodists attended the following Sunday's worship service, instead of the usual 36.[188]

March 2008: A Methodist congregation in Smolensk had its Sunday school, attended by four children, dissolved by the Regional Court on 24th March. The court said the Sunday school was unlicensed.[189]

Feature: Pope's 81st Birthday Broadcast to Russia

Address on state television wins support from across Russia

ACN (UK) News, April 2008[190]

A BROADCAST by Pope Benedict XVI on Russian state television has been hailed as a landmark in Orthodox–Catholic relations.

There has been widespread praise for the programme which featured a biography of the Pope and ended with a short address by the Pope.

Sources close to the Russian Orthodox Church expressed support for the broadcast and the text of the Pope's address has appeared on Sedmitza, an official website of the Church.

Meantime, the initiative's organisers described receiving "nothing but very positive feedback" from people who saw the programme on the Vesti news channel on the afternoon of 16th April and again early the following morning.

Speaking a few days after the broadcast, Peter Humeniuk, Russia expert for *Aid to the Church in Need*, which funded the initiative, said he was "a little shocked" by the positive reaction to the programme.

Stressing that it was "still early days" since the broadcast, he said: "What we have heard so far is that viewers found Pope Benedict honest and warm. They thought he was a person of great dignity and also enormous sympathy."

Mr Humeniuk, who spearheaded the initiative, said: "Even the enemies of Catholicism were, I think, a bit surprised to see this presentation of the Pope and how sympathetic a person he is."

Timed for release on the Pope's birthday, the broadcast – part of which was in Russian – shows Pope Benedict XVI highlighting the importance of Church unity.

The Pope continues: "Both the Catholic Church and the Russian Orthodox Church are moving in this direction."

He pays tribute to Christians in Russia – both Catholic and Orthodox – describing how over the past 100 years "the shadows of suffering and violence were opposed and overcome by the splendid light of so many martyrs, who perished under the oppression of ferocious persecutions."

Broadcast to about two-thirds of Russia on Wednesday (16th April) afternoon, the 30-minute programme had huge exposure. Many viewers were from outside Russia with Vesti being described as equivalent to the BBC World Service.

A second, longer version of the broadcast went out on Vesti a few hours later at 1am Moscow time on Thursday (17th April).

Stressing the significance of the programme's success, the initiative's organisers described how for years the Catholic Church had been criticised in Russia, with particular criticism directed against the papacy.

Relations between Rome and Moscow have developed significantly since 2002, when the Russian Orthodox hierarchy expressed alarm after the creation of four Catholic dioceses in Russia.

Pope Benedict's book *An Introduction to Christianity*, written when he was a university professor, was published in Russian last year, complete with a foreword by Metropolitan Kirill, of Smolensk and Kaliningrad, chairman of the External Church Relations Department of the Moscow Patriarchate.

Mr Humeniuk underlined the importance of Benedict XVI's personal contribution to the programme, describing how his brilliance as a theologian and a thinker is respected in Moscow and has roots dating back to his involvement in the Second Vatican Council.

Mr Humeniuk added: "The broadcast is the latest in a series of positive signs that suggest that the dialogue between Moscow and Rome is becoming more intensive."

The success of the broadcast is likely to increase speculation of a long-awaited meeting between Pope Benedict XVI and Alexei II, the Moscow-based Russian Orthodox Patriarch.

Saudi Arabia

Population	Religions	Christian Population
25 million	Muslim 95% Christian 3.5% Other 1.5%	800,000

In Saudi Arabia religious freedom is emphatically rejected, even in principle. The kingdom declares itself to be "integrally" Islamic and regards the *Qur'an* as the country's only constitution and the *Shari'a* as its basic law. According to the version of Wahabism endorsed by the state, the fact that the Arabic peninsula was the prophet Mohammed's homeland raises huge difficulties for the practice of other faiths, even the 'religions of the book' – Judaism and Christianity. Declaring Saudi Arabia to be a country of "particular concern", the US Department of State recently noted that while recognising the right of non-Muslims to worship in private, the regime "does not always respect this practice and does not define this right in law".[191]

In practice, anything that might be deemed an 'attack' against Islam is severely prosecuted and the authorities seek to prevent the spread of any other religion. Every expression of non-Muslim faith (including possession of Bibles, wearing a crucifix and praying in public) is forbidden.

The religious police (*mutawwa'in*) wield enormous power and monitor non-Muslim activities. They prosecute people caught drinking alcohol, those flouting the Islamic dress code, and anyone involved in 'immoral' behaviour. They clamp down on all religious activities – even private ones – not in compliance with *Wahabi* Islam. In its first report, the National Society for Human Rights accused the *mutawwa'in* of violations including "obtaining confessions through force".

It is difficult to calculate the total Christian population in Saudi Arabia. What is clear is that they make up a surprisingly large proportion of the country's foreign work force of more than eight million. Best guesses put the figure at less than one million. They are mainly from the Philippines, but also from Europe, the United States and the Middle East. Christians are deprived of all pastoral care, since priests are not allowed into the country. Reports show that the Filipino community in the capital, Riyadh, has been worst hit by a recent *mutawwa'in* crackdown on Christian services.

84

May 2007: A Saudi citizen was reportedly arrested for converting to Christianity. The only reports available suggest he was tortured.

August 2007: The case of a Christian doctor of Egyptian origin called Mamdooh Fahmy was resolved when he was finally allowed to return to Cairo. Starting in 2004, his colleagues in the hospital where he worked insulted him for being a Christian. The *mutawwa'in* then searched his home and accused him of being a Christian missionary and of drinking alcohol. After five days in isolation, he was released. Having lost his job, he wanted to return to Egypt, but for two years the Saudi authorities refused to return his passport or provide him with documents necessary to leave the country. The case was finally resolved, partly thanks to a campaign led by *International Christian Concern*.

November 2007: Pope Benedict XVI welcomed Saudi King Abdallah to Rome. In the absence of diplomatic relations, this was the first such meeting between the Holy See and Saudi Arabia. The Vatican has long held concerns about religious freedom in Saudi Arabia. *Al Jazeera* TV network stated that the issues discussed included the "situation experienced by the Christian minority in Saudi Arabia, the need for greater interreligious cooperation and prospects for peace in the Middle East".

April 2008: Saudi Arabia's Grand Mufti Anwar Ashiqi spoke out against plans for the first church to be built in Saudi Arabia in modern times. During his November 2007 meeting in Rome with Saudi King Abdullah, Benedict XVI inquired about plans for the church. He noted that as of Easter 2008 Qatar would have a church, making Saudi Arabia the only country in the Arab Peninsula without an official public place of Christian worship. King Abdullah promised to consider the plans. But later, Grand Mufti Anwar Ashiqi gave an interview, stating: "It would be possible to launch official negotiations to construct a church in Saudi Arabia only after the Pope and all the Christian churches recognise the prophet Mohammed."[192]

Sri Lanka

Population	Religions	Christian Pop.
19.5 million	Buddhist 70% Muslim 7.5% Hindu 7% Christian 9%, Other 6.5%	1.75 million

The situation in Sri Lanka deteriorated badly in 2006 and 2007 following a return to civil war. Clashes between separatist movement the Liberation Tigers of Tamil Eelam (LTTE) and government security forces climaxed with a series of attacks and suicide bombs against civilians in the south and the capital, Colombo. Churches in the north-east quickly became yet another casualty of war. The human cost of the conflict is high: since 1983, 70,000 people have died in the civil war; 5,000 in 2007 alone.[193]

Sri Lanka's constitution gives Buddhism the "foremost place", but provides religious freedom for all faiths. And yet, the Christian minority has been targeted by Buddhist extremists. Undaunted, the Church continues to be a leading voice denouncing human rights violations perpetrated by both sides. Churches are calling for a diplomatic solution to the 25-year conflict.

While two anti-conversion bills before parliament were shelved, the Act for the Protection of Religious Freedom is still waiting for a reading. The act would impose a prison term of up to seven years and a large fine for people guilty of trying to "convert or attempt to convert, either directly or otherwise, any person from one religion to another". The legislation would create separate Buddhist courts – independent of state courts – with power to rule on petitions forwarded by villagers.

Bishop Joseph Fernando of Kandy, chairman of the Catholic Bishops' Conference, has said: "Fundamentalist Christian groups over the past 20 years have exploited conditions of poverty and people's needs to aggressively convert them. Such behaviour has greatly upset the Buddhist majority but has also been a cause for concern for the Church itself since Catholics have been the most affected by it." In attacking Christians, Buddhists make no distinction between different religious denominations.

In their bid to stop the draft law, Sri Lanka's Catholic bishops have called on Christian fundamentalists to stop trying to convert people by "unethical" means. Catholics and Protestants have worked together to oppose the bill, joining forces with Muslims, Hindus and some Buddhist leaders.

Catholic leaders have made several appeals to the Vatican to put pressure on Sri Lankan authorities to respect human rights and religious freedom. They have called for the "release" of Sri Lanka's northern Jaffna peninsula, after the government cut off land routes. When Sri Lankan President Mahinda Rajapakse visited the Vatican on 20th April 2007, the Justice and Peace Commission of Jaffna sent a letter to the Pope calling for the reopening of Highway A9 "even under the control of an international monitoring team" since it is the only link between Jaffna and the rest of the island and the only way in for humanitarian aid. Noting the large number of people who have disappeared, the letter appealed for the matter to be investigated by observers from the UN Human Rights Commission. In 2006 alone 583 people disappeared. The Pope urged a diplomatic solution to the conflict, speaking out four times between mid-2006 and 2007.

September 2007: Father Nicholaspilai Packiyaranjith was killed when a mine exploded under his car as he was making his way with food and other necessities to the refugee camp and an orphanage in Vidathalvu. The 40-year-old priest worked as the coordinator for the Jesuit Refugee Services in Mannar district. No one claimed responsibility for the attack.

October 2007: Catholics from Rosa Mystica Church in Kotugoda Parish in Crooswatta – made up of 300 families – were too afraid to attend Mass and catechism classes, fearing violence from Buddhist extremists. The church itself was built in 2003 and extension work began in February 2007. Reports stated that in September 2007 the head of a nearby Buddhist temple, Uddammita Buddahsiri, protested against the extension. He said: "If building does not stop by tomorrow, you'll lose 10 to 15 lives."
Parish priest Father Susith Silva went to court where the judge temporarily suspended the building work and appealed to both sides to settle the dispute amicably. The parish obeyed the injunction, but on 6th October, police interrupted Mass and told the priest to stop the service. The Catholic families, mostly farmers, cannot afford the taxi fare to reach other churches, the nearest of which is several miles away. Hence, they returned to court calling for the religious activities to be resumed and assumed the church construction matter would be settled at a later date. Local Buddhists reacted by protesting that this was an insult to the 348 Buddhist families

living nearby. Buddhist leader Uddammita said: "We are not going to let them finish the building. If it restarts, the whole village is going to rise up."

December 2007: Bishop Thomas Savundaranayagam of Jaffna criticised police for not doing enough in the search for Fr Thiruchchelvan Nihal Jim Brown, 35, and layman Wenceslaus Vinces Vimalathas, who disappeared in August 2006. The two men were last seen at a military checkpoint in Allapiddy, where Fr Brown is parish priest. Allapiddy is a village in an island off the Sri Lankan coast, an area tightly controlled by the Sri Lankan navy. Soon after their disappearance, human rights campaigners *Amnesty International* raised concerns that the two men were taken into custody, claims strongly denied by Colombo. More than 15 months later and with no sign of any break-through, Bishop Savundaranayagam accused the authorities of "procrastinating" in their search for the two men. He told *UCA News*: "The state is not conducting the inquiry with sincerity."[194]

February 2008: Two men shot the Rev. Samson Neil Edirisinghe, 37, killing him instantly, and left his wife Shiromi, 31, in a critical condition. The couple's two-year-old son received minor injuries and suffered shock after witnessing the attack on his parents. It was a contract killing arranged by a local Buddhist nationalist angered by Pastor Edirisinghe's ministry.[195]

April 2008: Father M. X. Karunaratnam, parish priest of Vavunikkulam, in the Jaffna diocese, was killed in a landmine blast at Ambalkulam on his return home from Mass. The priest was the founder and chairman of the North East Secretariat on Human Rights, a group that reports on rights issues related to minority ethnic Tamils.[196]

May 2008: The Sri Lankan Defence Ministry announced plans to designate a "security zone" around the shrine of Our Lady of Madhu. Army Commander Lt. Gen. Sarath Fonseka said the shrine, which was damaged due to shelling in the past few months, was now under government control and would be handed back to the Church. Father Surenthiran Ravel Leenus, secretary of the Bishop of Mannar, said the shrine's statue of Our Lady could only be returned if a one-mile quarantine was imposed around it. The statue was removed in April during heavy fighting and taken for safe-keeping to St. Francis Xavier Church in Thevanpiti, a coastal village where 20,000 displaced people were living in camps or with relatives.[197]

Sudan

Population	Religions	Christian Population
38 million	Muslim 72% Christian 14% Animist 12% Other 2%	5.5 million

The jailing of Gillian Gibbons, a British primary school teacher working in Khartoum, revealed the scale of religious freedom abuses in Sudan. Ms Gibbons, from Liverpool, received a 15-day prison term in November 2007 for offences against the prophet of Islam after allowing a teddy bear to be named Mohammed in a school competition. She narrowly escaped receiving 40 lashes. Pressure on the Khartoum government was already intense amid the continued humanitarian crisis in Darfur, a region with comparatively few Christians. Within a few days of her imprisonment, Sudan President Omar al-Bashir was forced to intervene and release Ms Gibbons before her prison term had run its course.

The incident, in the capital, Khartoum, points to the growing gulf in terms of religious tolerance opening up between northern Sudan and the south. The latter was ceded local control as part of a six-year programme set out in the January 2005 Comprehensive Peace Agreement. In the 10 regions of southern Sudan, freedom of worship is guaranteed as a principle of government.

However in the north citizens are subject to *Shari'a* Islamic law, as interpreted by the National Congress Party. Muslim women are banned from marrying Christian men and alcohol is forbidden. These are just some of a series of laws, some of which theoretically carry extreme sentences such as corporal punishment including mutilation of limbs.

But the main problem for Christians and other non-Muslims is the strict ban on apostasy. In theory, offences of this kind carry the death penalty. The ban puts people at grave risk of being accused of encouraging Muslims to abandon their faith. Religious organisations in northern Sudan, including the Churches, are obliged to restrict their activities to ensure they do not attract people from other faiths.

The problems are compounded by the vulnerability of many Christians. In Khartoum, hundreds of thousands live in displacement camps having escaped the south during the civil war of 1983-2004. Addressing the rights of non-Muslims in Khartoum, Sudan's President Omar al-Bashir set up a commission in February 2007 but reports claimed little progress had been made. One key break-through however has been the release of more than 840 women imprisoned with their 160 children for alcohol production and distribution offences. For 30 years the state refused all permissions for the construction of churches until finally the Ministry for Planning and Public Property approved the erection of three church buildings near Khartoum. Other churches, built without planning permission, have been partially destroyed.

Meantime, in south Sudan, despite the rise of a regional government, Church leaders have repeatedly claimed that the Khartoum government is intent on Islamization. They claim people have been pressurised into becoming Muslims through a vast system of schools, hospitals and other welfare support structures funded by Islamist organisations. Aid is desperately needed in this massively deprived region still recovering from a civil war which claimed up to three million lives.

2007: The US State Department Report on International Religious Freedom criticised the authorities in Khartoum. It states that Christians in northern Sudan repeatedly complained about social discrimination both in schools and in the work-place. The State government and local authorities in northern Sudan applied pressure on Church leaders to give up property in central Khartoum dating back to the colonial era (before 1957). The government was also reported as refusing the Church permission to build on its own land. Khartoum stated they wanted to buy the land from church leaders for redevelopment.[198]

January 2007: Auxiliary Bishop Daniel Adwok Kur of Khartoum spoke out against the Khartoum government, accusing it of "playing games" with the people. He said Khartoum was not committed to the Comprehensive Peace Agreement, signed with south Sudan leaders two years earlier. The bishop said the government had failed to help internally displaced people – many of them Christians – return to their homelands in the south. He said government treatment of non-Muslims in the Khartoum area remained very poor. But he praised the Khartoum authorities for granting permission for the erection of three churches in the area, the first authorisation of its kind given to the Catholic Church in 30 years.[199]

90

January 2007: Police officers used tear gas to attack an Episcopalian church in Khartoum diocese. Inside were 800 people attending a New Year's Eve prayer vigil. Among those present was Sudan Vice President Abel Alier. Six people were injured. Damage to the church was estimated at US$7,000. No action was taken against the police officers.[200]

April 2007: A man wearing the uniform of the Sudanese People's Liberation Army/Movement (south Sudan political/military movement) blew himself up during an open-air religious event near a Baptist Church in Khorfulus, in the Upper Nile region. Six children were killed in the attack and five were wounded.[201]

April 2007: An Egyptian named Daniel Girgis, aged 37, and Sudanese Markous Tiya, Rihab Kafi Jadeen, and another unidentified young man, all Evangelical Christians, were assassinated after holding a Christian catechetical class in the Nuba Mountains. The four were members of the Bahry Evangelical Church in Khartoum. The assassins were not identified but, according to local sources, suspicion fell on Islamic fundamentalists, irritated by the evangelical activities of the Christian group.

May 2007: Speaking to *Aid to the Church in Need*, Bishop Adwok of Khartoum said that the Khartoum government was using the Darfur crisis as a smokescreen for the spread of Islam into the mainly Christian south. In an ACN interview given ahead of his keynote address at an ACN conference in Glasgow, Scotland, the bishop said Khartoum was working with Islamic organisations in the Middle East to fund mosques, schools and hospitals all with the specific aim of evangelisation. Once again questioning the government's commitment to the 2005 peace agreement and its commitment to religious freedom, he said: "The government is ringing the same bell of Islamizing Sudan while at the same time talking about the importance of the CPA."[202]

June 2007: Adam Adam, a humanitarian worker for a relief organisation connected with Churches Together, a partner of Caritas, was killed by three armed men. He was one of the leaders of the refugee camp in Khamsa Degaig, near Zalingei, west of Darfur, and home to 100,000 displaced people.

September 2007: Five young people were killed in a suicide attack by a militant member of the Sudan People's Liberation Army (SPLA). The terrorist released a grenade after walking into a church in Khorfulus, 30 miles south-west of Malakal, in the Upper Nile state. The dead were named as: Donguei Matok Chan, aged eight, Dhieu Nyandual, 20, Nyaniok Ryak Chol Ayoum, 11, Nyawyly Kon Rwaj, 11, and 17-year-old Simon Chol Charles Thon Arob.

November 2007: Gillian Gibbons, a teacher from Liverpool, UK, working in a primary school in Khartoum, was arrested after a colleague reported her for insulting Islam. She was accused of allowing a child in her class of seven-year-olds to name a teddy bear Mohammed in a school competition. She was tried immediately and sentenced to 15 days in prison. Islamic authorities and protest groups demanded that she receive 40 lashes and six months in prison. After an international outcry, on 4th December she was pardoned by President Omar al-Bashir and was deported back to the UK.[203]

June 2008: *International Christian Concern* (ICC) announced that up to 90 percent of homes in the disputed oil-rich region of Abeyi were burned down in new clashes between government troops and the Sudanese Peoples Liberation Army/Movement (SPLA/M). The compound of the Catholic church was also attacked. The conflict forced up to 80,000 southern Sudanese residents to leave the disputed area. According to ICC, northern Sudanese troops have taken control of Abeyi in direct violation of the Comprehensive Peace Agreement (CPA) of 2005. They predict that the conflict would create a new humanitarian crisis. In an ICC interview, Ruben Benjamin reported: "70-80,000 people are now living in the bush surrounding Abeyi – kids and women – they need quick humanitarian help."[204]

Profile: Bishop Giorgio Bertin

Bishop of Djibouti and Apostolic Administrator of Somalia[205]

"I do not want to offer my head on a plate too easily. If martyrdom does eventually come, I ask for the strength to go through with it."

Martyrdom and missionary work go hand-in-hand in the life of Bishop Giorgio Bertin.

As the Italian Franciscan began to speak, the swarm of flies and the oppressive heat were soon forgotten as he described the drama of life as a bishop in this corner of the Horn of Africa overlooking the south-west corner of Arabia.

The Italian Franciscan is one of the only Church leaders ministering in Somalia, a war-torn country and scene of one of Africa's worst humanitarian crises.

When the Somali capital Mogadishu was overthrown by Islamic militants in the early 1990s, all 12 churches were attacked, including the cathedral.

The then Father Giorgio had worked in Somalia for some years and was forced to flee as lawlessness overran the country.

Now he's back – if not on a full-time basis. Not only is he Bishop of Djibouti but he is also administrator apostolic of Somalia, stepping in after his predecessor was killed.

Bishop Bertin and his vicar general share out their duties, travelling hours on end on a Sunday to say Mass at out-stations all over the region.

Once, when the Bishop's car broke down in northern Somalia, he celebrated the liturgy by himself both on Good Friday and Holy Saturday.

He explained that his faith was a powerful call to action even if he couldn't always measure it in concrete results.

"It's a question of attitude," he adds, pensively. "If you do not change your attitude, even a forest can seem like a desert. Here you are challenged to live your Christian faith at a very deep level."

Catholics in the region are few in number – many are in hiding. Recently he visited the region of Somalia that was part of British Somaliland. "There are very few refugees working in NGOs," he said. "They are very afraid to come to church."

He said his work is discreet. Consolata missionary Sister Leonella Sgorbati was killed in Mogadishu in September 2006, an event linked by many to the Muslim outrage following Pope Benedict XVI's Regensburg speech in Germany.

For Bishop Bertin, who presided at Sister Sgorbati's funeral, the Pope's speech was "the straw that broke the camel's back", a sign of the underlying antagonism to Christianity and its perceived close links with the West.

Nor was the violence confined to Somalia. Pointing to chips in the brickwork in his office, he explained how the outrage over Regensburg prompted youths to throw stones at him. In an ironic twist, he pointed at a selection of the stones in question, which he keeps as a "souvenir".

He is determined not to be coerced into submission. He produces a radio programme on Vatican Radio on Saturday evenings with extracts from Scripture and accompanying commentary.

In Djibouti, the Church still runs 10 schools. He says: "The schools are a principal tool to show our evangelising presence."

Reliant on support from a range of agencies, he has received help from *Aid to the Church in Need* to repair his cathedral, vehicles to visit far-flung faithful and copies of ACN's Child's Bible translated by the bishop into Somali.

Hope is a constant theme for Bishop Bertin. He concluded, saying: "Over the past decades, the Church has shared all the good moments, and bad – all the triumphs and trials – of the people of Somalia. The martyrs, including Sister Leonella, demonstrate that this is true."

Turkey

Population	Religions	Christian Population
74.5 million	Muslim 97% Atheist 2.5% Christian 0.5%	500,000

During his long-awaited trip to Turkey in late 2006, Pope Benedict XVI highlighted the importance of religious freedom, implicitly referring to the growth of anti-Christian sentiment. He spoke of Christians now being perceived as "internal enemies". Such tensions have been the seed-bed for the attacks against Christians that took place in 2007.

The constitution describes Turkey as a "democratic, secular and social State that respects human rights" (Article 2), one that allows "total freedom of conscience and religious persuasion" (Article 24). However, Turkey places religion under the auspices of the *Dyanet*, which manages religious affairs. All those with jobs related to religion (teachers of religion, ministers, etc) depend on this department for their appointment, training and salaries. Jews and Christians are not represented on the *Dyanet*. In the name of secularism, denominational minorities cannot be represented in parliament.

The Jewish community, the Greek Orthodox Church, and the Armenian Apostolic Church are recognised by the 1923 Treaty of Lausanne. They are guaranteed the same legal rights as other citizens of Turkish origin (Article 40). However, the authorities have always implemented its provisions in a restrictive way. A 1935 law requiring religious institutions to submit an inventory of their possessions is used to justify the arbitrary closure of church buildings. Christians not covered by the Treaty of Lausanne do not have any legal status or rights, and cannot legally own or manage their own schools, social centres or seminaries, nor can they build churches.[206]

January 2007: A Protestant church in Samsun was attacked by an anonymous group who smashed the building's windows with stones.[207]

April 2007: Five young Muslims entered the Christian publishing house *Zirve* in the south-eastern province of Malatya and cut the throats of three Protestants. Two of the victims were Christian converts, Necati Aydin and Ugur Yuksel, and the other was a German, Tilmann Geske. The accused were caught at the scene of the crime, with butcher's knives in their hands and the blood of the victims on their clothing. The publishing house distributed Bibles and other Christian literature.[208]

July 2007: A state prosecutor demanded a serious punishment for two Christians on trial for "insulting Turkishness", which became a crime under Article 301 of the Penal Code in 2005. Muslim converts to Christianity Hakan Tastan and Turan Topal were accused of cursing Turkey and Islam as well as forcing people to convert.[209]

September 2007: Police in the city of Izmit, north-west Turkey, arrested Semih Sahin, who started a fire at the entrance of the local Protestant church before firing his gun several times. The minister of the Church is the brother-in-law of one of the men murdered in Malatya.[210]

October 2007: Soner Tufan, director of Radio Shema, a Christian station in the Turkish capital, Ankara, said that at least three times a month men came to the station's door and threatened workers.[211]

November 2007: Forest rangers began demolishing the 17th century chapel of the Transfiguration of the Lord, next to a seminary. They removed tiles from the roof and broke all the windows and fixtures. The complete destruction of the chapel was only averted at the last minute, following protests to the local prefect.

December 2007: Italian Capuchin Father Adriano Francini, 65, was hospitalised after he was stabbed outside the Church of Saint Anthony in Smyrna. His attacker, a 19-year-old Muslim man, justified his crime saying that the priest had refused to baptise him. (Pretending to be a candidate for baptism is a method frequently used to accuse Christians of proselytism). According to the newspaper, *Hurriyet*, the perpetrator told police he had been influenced by a recent episode of the television series *Kurtlar Vadisi* (Valley of the Wolves), which depicts Christian missionaries as political 'infiltrators' who pay poor families to convert to Christianity.[212]

January 2008: In the Black Sea coastal city of Samsun, Judge Sinan Sonmez freed 17-year-old Semih Seymen, who admitted to making several threats to kill a pastor named Orhan Picaklar. The judge decided to free him a day after his arrest "because of his youth".[213]

Uzbekistan

Population	Religions	Christian Population
27.4 million	Muslim 88% Orthodox 9% Other 3%	2.5 million

The US State Department added Uzbekistan to its list of "Countries of Particular Concern" in 2006. While its constitution guarantees freedom of religion (Articles 18, 31 and 61), religious freedom was restricted by new laws in 1998. In June 2006 penalties were introduced targeting "the illegal production, conservation, importation and distribution of unauthorised religious literature". A proposed bill to outlaw discussing religious issues outside "recognised" places of worship, would fine offenders up to 600 times the average monthly salary (about US$10) for a first offence. Subsequent offences could lead to jail terms of eight years.[214]

Uzbekistan's secret police, the National Security Service (NSS), and the *mahallas* (neighbourhood-level administrations) are powerful tools for restricting religious activities. NSS agents carry out surveillance on places of worship and occasionally recruit infiltrators to inform on other worshippers and church activities, causing religious groups to be increasingly suspicious. Phones have been tapped: "Often when we talk on the phone for a long time about Christianity," said one Protestant leader, "a voice just tells us to stop talking and put the phone down."[215]

While the Orthodox Church does not face any specific problems, Uzbekistan's small Catholic Church is closely monitored and the registration of parishes is extremely difficult. Protestant communities endure police raids and groups worshipping in their homes are subject to legal penalties, including imprisonment. Protestants are seen as 'Western' and perceived as dangerous because they proselytise. A programme on Uzbek state television entitled "Hypocrites" accused them of coercing people to join: "On the pretext of financially helping people in need, they instil their own teachings in... people's minds... Soon the targeted people become complete zombies."[216] The claims were echoed by Professor Mansur Bekmuradov of the Tashkent State Institute of Culture who said evangelization was tantamount to "religious violence".[217]

The government has clamped down on human rights groups suspected of ties with religious groups or receiving aid from the West. In 2006 a court suspended more than 10 such associations. Authorities in Tashkent shut down the NGO Central Asia Free Exchange (CAFÉ) after a court found its members guilty of unlawful proselytism. The group, which trained medical staff, built orphanages and taught English, was also charged with the unlicensed use of the Internet and using an unauthorised logo.

April 2007: A pastor's daughter was kidnapped. She was traumatised by the ordeal as her family discovered on her release. They received threats and beatings, allegedly inspired by the mullahs at the local mosque. [218]

June 2007: Sharofat Allamova was charged for possessing Christian literature. She was discovered with Christian books in her bag while on a bus taking her back to her home town of Urgench. In September, she was convicted of breaking religion laws which carry a maximum sentence of three years' imprisonment. She was given a suspended sentence. [219]

July 2007: Pentecostals Hudoer Pardaev and Igor Kim spent 10 days in prison after they were judged guilty of holding "illegal" religious classes.

September 2007: Protestant Pastor Khyn-Mun Kim, was fined a year's salary for "illegal" religious activity.[220]

January 2008: Uzbekistan authorities investigated claims that Grace Church was "hypnotising" people, and using "psychotropic substances," to "stupefy the minds of our children", after a series of articles in state-run newspaper, *Narodnoe Slovomade*s. Criminal charges were dropped after it was proved untrue that a cough medicine had mind-altering qualities.[221]

March 2008: A Baptist in Fergana city was fined nine months' wages after his home was raided. 40 people took part in a Sunday service there.[222]

May 2008: A Protestant student was threatened with expulsion, unless he renounced his faith or spied on his church for the NSS. Police also told Baptist school children that they would be jailed if they went to church. [223]

July 2008: Uzbekistan's Bible Society was refused permission for a shipment of 11,000 Bibles and related books to clear through customs.[224]

Venezuela

Population	Religions	Christian Population
27.7 million	Catholic 96% Protestant 2% Other 2%	27 million

President Hugo Chavez is bringing about the 'Bolivarian Revolution' – the introduction of neo-Marxist principles – at a time when the country is experiencing poverty and financial insecurity. Chavez's reforms involve institutional changes throughout the country. One key example is the introduction of 'Bolivarian Circles', loose-knit political and social organisations of workers' councils. These circles help the government identify opponents, who are then denied public services.[225]

Tension is increasing between government institutions and the Church, partly because of the Chavez socialist experiment. When the Catholic bishops insisted that Chavez's reforms uphold civil liberties,[226] the President accused them of fomenting rebellion. The bishops defended the right to freedom of speech and described Chavez's provocations as an attempt to distract people from the country's real problems.[227] The Episcopal conference urged that the country be open to spiritual values, avoiding a form of Marxist socialism with totalitarian tendencies.[228] Chavez responded by accusing the Catholic hierarchy of "talking nonsense", and advised them to read Marx, Lenin, and the Sermon on the Mount to discover the true inspiration of socialism.[229]

The tension was also visible in issues such as the bishops' defence of freedom of expression following the closure of the television channel *Canal Radio Caracas de Television*.[230] In July 2007, the bishops criticised Chavez's constitutional reforms for being undemocratic; and highlighted the increase in poverty and unemployment and the restriction of freedom of expression. They said a new education law failed to give parents the right to request religious education in schools.[231] Cardinal Jorge Urosa, the Archbishop of Caracas, underlined the dangers of state-run education even if it differed from the Bolivarian model.[232] He said the Church would doggedly oppose the so-called "Socialism of the 21st century" if it proved to be similar to old-style communist regimes.[233] Other bishops echoed his views.[234]

August 2007: The bishops published an exhortation: "Called to live in freedom" ("Llamados a vivir en la libertad"), in which they said the planned constitutional reform was an attack on democracy and human rights.[235] The bishops' comments provoked ferocious criticism from the government, which increased in the run-up to a referendum on the reforms. Chavez accused the Church of manipulation and lying[236] and called Cardinal Oscar Rodriguez Madariaga, Archbishop of Tegucigalpa, Honduras, an "imperialist clown".[237]

November 2007: Just days before the referendum on constitutional reform, seminarians from one diocese sent a letter to the bishops' conference, declaring their loyalty to both the hierarchy and the Church's social teachings. In their letter, they stated that their loyalty was crucial "at this so decisive moment in the history of the country". The seminarians echoed the bishops' view that the reforms were "morally unacceptable" and "irreconcilable with the Christian faith and its view of man and society". They thanked the bishops for having warned "emphatically and without hesitation" of this danger. The letter goes on: "We know from history of the tragic fate of countries that have lived under a Socialist regime where the state holds absolute sway over the individual." And later, it states: "We regard it as a threat to democracy when violent, physical or verbal means are used against those who express their views openly."[238]

December 2007: The Archdiocese of Caracas rejected accusations by Vice President Jorge Rodriguez that the Catholic Church was sponsoring political meetings opposing the constitutional reforms and had provided a venue for them to take place. Cardinal Jorge Urosa Savino, Archbishop of Caracas, explained that the meeting was an initiative of the laity that had taken place in a community centre which is not parish property.[239] Shortly afterwards, the cardinal was physically attacked by a gang of about 15 members of the government group, *La esquina caliente*. Police were accused of failing to act despite being close to the scene of the attack.[240]

July 2008: Archbishop Antonio José López Castillo of Barquisimeto criticised the Chavez regime's attitude to the Church: "The government regards the Church as 'the Opium of the people' and has publicly described it as 'a cancer in society'... In every sphere, [the government] is trying to insinuate that the Church is not close to the people." He added that more recently the government was showing signs of being "more moderate".[241]

Vietnam

Population	Religions	Christian Population
87 million	None 81% Buddhist 9% Christian 7.5% Other 2.5 %	6.5 million

A new religious law came into effect in February 2007, which treats the country's different faiths as social forces that can and must contribute to its progress, under the guidance of the Communist Party. Religious activities are subject to the scrutiny of the civil authorities. For example, at the start of each year religious leaders must submit an annual plan of activities for state approval. Recently, the bishops have only had to inform the authorities about activities such as pilgrimages, diocesan gatherings, etc. Generally, the authorities do not refuse these activities any more but there are some exceptions. The law allows nuns and priests to work as individual citizens in education, the media, and health care. But it bans religious organisations from doing so.

The level of religious freedom is directly related to what local authorities are willing to allow. What the authorities do if they want to be troublesome is to create all kinds of nuisances and obstacles to daily work: for example, withholding permissions for all manner of activities, allowing noisy activities close to monasteries and refusing to recognise new religious communities. Most Catholics are able to go about their business without interruption. They no longer fear arrests or physical abuse.

The US and the Holy See have acknowledged that the situation has improved in the country. The State Department removed Vietnam from its list of countries of particular concern over religious freedom. A Vatican press release (25th January 2007), marking the first meeting between Vietnam's Prime Minister Nguyễn Tấn Dũng and Pope Benedict XVI, stated: "Relations have, over the last few years, made concrete progress, opening new spaces of religious freedom for the Catholic Church in Vietnam." However, the statement also referred to unspecified "problems that remain" which can hopefully be resolved "through existing channels of dialogue". Vietnam's tightly controlled press reported that the prime minister had mentioned a possible restoration of normal diplomatic relations with the Vatican after a break of more than 50 years. This same idea was reflected in a Vatican statement of March 2007.

January 2007: 17 people were arrested at a prayer meeting organised by the Mennonite Church at the home of Rev Nguyen Hong Quang.[242]

March 2007: Catholic priest Father Nguyen Van Ly received an eight-year jail term after being accused of being a founding member of pro-democracy movement Bloc 8406, and being a member of the Progression Party of Vietnam. The state allows only the Communist Party to exist. Father Van Ly was arrested when security officers surrounded his church as he prepared for Mass. By then, Father Van Ly had already spent 14 of the past 24 years in prison and he had been under house arrest since February. The US House of Representatives called for his "unconditional release".[243]

August 2007: A school denied an eleven-year-old Christian student, Phong Hong, the right to sit its entrance exam because of a new rule barring "students who follow a religion". Tran Van Ha, principal of Ka Dang Public Elementary School in Quang Nam province, wrote to Phong's parents saying that the decision was beyond his control.[244]

January 2008: Around 50 Catholics from Ploi Hamong Ktu village, in Dak Ha district, were holding prayers when they were stopped by police. Four of them, one adult and three teenagers, were detained and beaten by security forces. The teenagers were whipped with bamboo sticks, kicked and slapped in the face. The police repeatedly kicked a 43-year-old man and gave him electric shocks until he lost consciousness. He was left on the ground, bleeding and remained unconscious for more than an hour. Some weeks later, he was still unable to walk.[245]

February 2008: The government promised the Catholic Church that it would return the former apostolic nunciature building in the Vietnamese capital, Hanoi. Archbishop Ngô Quang Kiêt confirmed this development after Vatican Secretary of State Cardinal Tarcisio Bertone sent him a letter stating that Rome would raise the issue with the government. This followed clashes with police and protestors at the former nunciature in early January. At the time, Vietnamese-language newspapers and TV stations attacked the Church for its demands (25th January). By contrast, the international edition of *Nham Dam*, the Communist Party's official newspaper, provided a more positive view of the Church when it reported on Archbishop Ngô's meeting with Patriotic Front chairman Huỳnh Đảm, ostensibly to exchange greetings for the start of the Lunar New Year (7th February). The paper also provided an overview of the Church's humanitarian activities and other work in the capital. It also mentioned the Patriotic Front's "appreciation" for their activities.[246]

February 2008: Officials arrested 15 Hmong Christian families in the Bokeo district of Laos, which borders Vietnam. Eight Christian families were bundled into six trucks which arrived in Ban Sai Jarern village. Authorities also arrested at least seven families from nearby Fai village. A Christian source said: "It seems they are rounding up all Hmong Christians from Laos to send them back to Vietnam. What will happen to them is greatly feared and unknown." Nine church leaders sentenced for holding Christian services on 23rd February were rounded up during a police and military sweep of suspected rebels in July 2007 that left at least 13 Christians dead. The Christians were widely reported to have no connections with rebels.[247]

March 2008: A prayer appeal by the Evangelical Church of Vietnam (South) claimed the government had ignored peaceful attempts to win back confiscated church properties and put an end to interference in church affairs and discrimination against Christians. Addressed to "The Church of God Everywhere," the appeal letter from the Executive Committee of the Church followed several ultimatums in which the church threatened "collective action" but were still ignored by authorities. The Church received full legal recognition in April 2001 and is Vietnam's largest Protestant Church. The letter said some of the 265 confiscated properties had been used for other purposes. Others had been left to fall into disrepair or were demolished.[248]

May 2008: About 200 riot police and soldiers equipped with electrical batons and tear gas surrounded the village of Ploi Rwai, in Gialai province. This followed two meetings between the security police and members of house churches, who had been told that they must stop conducting religious services in their home and worship with the Evangelical Church of Vietnam. Church leader R'com H'Glah, aged 43, was arrested and imprisoned for refusing to join the state-approved Evangelical Church.[249]

Zimbabwe

Population	Religions	Christian Population
13 million	Christian 68% Animist 30% Other 2%	9 million

With its economy in tatters and its people devastated by poverty and mass unemployment, the crisis engulfing Zimbabwe has touched the lives of almost everybody in the country. In July 2008, inflation was conservatively estimated to be a record-breaking 2.2 million percent and was continuing to rise as shop prices increased by the hour. Repression and violence are commonplace in a country torn apart by conflict and the suffering has affected people whatever their religious beliefs.

The constitution guarantees religious liberty, but the government does not always respect this right. There is no state religion and all religions are recognised. Religious institutions do not have to be registered, unless they run schools or hospitals. Religious education is permitted in private schools.

Christian leaders who criticised the Mugabe regime have been threatened, arrested and even imprisoned. Senior clergy have been targeted, including the outspoken Archbishop Pius Ncube of Bulawayo. An April 2007 pastoral letter by Catholic bishops attacking "bad governance and corruption" in the country led to retaliation against the Church.[250] Priests were harassed and threatened by members of the government's Central Intelligence Organisation. Copies of the pastoral letter were confiscated and in some rural areas parishes were prohibited from reading the letter.[251]

The failure of President Robert Mugabe's ZANU-PF party to win the March 2008 elections caused outbreaks of violence, particularly in rural areas where support for the rival MDC party was high. In April 2008 Church leaders spoke out against the organised violence "unleashed" against people "accused of campaigning or voting for the 'wrong' political party" by the militia.[252] In urban areas armed police have bulldozed homes, leaving families living on the streets. One eye-witness of the events described it as "genocide in the making".[253]

When Mugabe won run-off presidential elections in June 2008, questions abounded about the legitimacy of the result. The outrage centred on news that Mugabe's opponent, Morgan Tsvangirai of the MDC, had withdrawn from the contest after fears that his supporters would be killed. In Mudzi, two polling stations reported 15,000 votes cast for Mugabe when only 3,000 people live in those wards.[254] The Southern African Development Community Observer Mission commented that events leading up to the polling day did not meet its election guidelines.

January 2007: Armed police arrested eight ministers at a meeting organised by the Zimbabwe Christian Alliance. The event was attended by more than 500 church leaders and lay people. The organisers notified the police as required under the law and several members of the Zimbabwe Republic Police sat in to monitor proceedings. The authorities claimed that the Christian Alliance incited the crowd to rise up against the government. The arrested men were released on bail two days later.[255]

May 2008: Catholic priests and lay people were among those being targeted by militia groups attacking those who voted against ZANU PF. A priest reported: "Many Catholic priests and lay people are on the wanted lists of these soldiers and militia groups, and many of them are forced to remain in hiding following death threats."[256]

May 2008: Police invoked security laws to ban open-air prayer meetings in some parts of the country in the run-up to the second round of presidential elections.[257]

May 2008: Worshippers were beaten or prevented from attending services as part of police attacks on churches across Harare. The violence comes after Nolbert Kunonga, the Anglican Bishop of Harare and a vocal supporter of Robert Mugabe, was replaced by Sebastian Bakare.[258]

[1] John Pontifex, Interview with Bishop Bertin, in Djibouti (February 2007), cited in *An Ancient Faith Renewed: Christians in Ethiopia and across the Horn of Africa*, ACN (UK) Report, Spring 2007.

[2] Ibid.

[3] *International Christian Concern*, Washington DC, USA; World Evangelical Alliance, *Report to UN Human Rights Commission 2007*; Dr Paul Marshall of the *Centre for Religious Freedom*, Washington.

[4] , World Evangelical Alliance, *Report to UN Human Rights Commission 2007*; Dr Paul Marshall of the *Centre for Religious Freedom*, Washington.

[5] *Religious Tolerance*, Ontario, Canada.

[6] *Christian Solidarity Worldwide* – Media office.

[7] David Aikman, *Jesus in Beijing* (Washington DC: Regnery Publishing, 2006), p. 21.

[8] Archbishop Lawrence Saldanha of Lahore, "Foreword", *Persecuted and Forgotten? A Report on Christians oppressed for their Faith 2005/2006*, (Sutton: ACN, 2006), p. 3.

[9] *ACN (UK) News*, 14.03.2008.

[10] Pope Benedict XVI, homily 07.04.2008 – marking the 40th anniversary of the Community of Sant' Edigio, held at a memorial to the 20th century martyrs on Tiber Island, Rome.

[11] Message marking ACN's 60th anniversary by Vatican Secretary of State Cardinal Tarcisio Bertone, read out to ACN staff at Castel Gandolfo, 16.09.2007.

[12] *Christian Today*, News, 31.05.2008.

[13] John Thavis, *Catholic Herald*, London, 27.06.2008.

[14] Pope Benedict XVI, Address at Castel Gandolfo marking ACN's 60th anniversary, 16.09.2007.

[15] Most total population figures following are taken from *BBC Country Profiles* (United Nations 2007). Other statistics are taken from *CIA World Fact Book,* 19.06.2008; *World Christian Encyclopedia*, 2001; (for Eritrea) *Nations Encyclopedia*; and (for Iraq) *Eglises du Monde*, no. 135, 3 (2007); occasionally amended or supplemented by ACN's own sources. Please note all figures are only approximate.

[16] *Christian Solidarity Worldwide*, CSW Briefing (Algeria), 03.2008.

[17] *Le Monde*, 26.02.2008.

[18] *La Croix*, 27.02.2008.

[19] *La Croix*, 03.09.2007.

[20] *Le Monde*, 26.02.2008.

[21] Ibid.

[22] Ibid.

[23] *Compass Direct News*, 17.03.2008; 28.03.2008.

[24] *International Christian Concern*, 29.05.2008; *The Tablet*, 07.06.2008.

[25] *Compass Direct News*, 10.04.2008.

[26] *International Christian Concern*, 29.05.2008.

[27] *Christian Today*, News, 31.05.2008.

[28] ACN (UK) interview – April 2008.

[29] *Catholic Hierarchy* website <http://www.catholic-hierarchy.org/diocese/dorna.html>.

[30] *Christian Solidarity Worldwide*, CSW Briefing, 10.03.2008.

[31] A movement springing from mainstream Islam in the late 19th century, originating with the life and teachings of Mirza Ghulam Ahmad (1835-1908).

[32] *ACN Newsflash*, 09.03.2007.

[33] *Compass Direct News*, 21.08.2007.

[34] *Compass Direct News*, 28.08.2007.
[35] *Compass Direct News*, 04.02.2008.
[36] *Forum 18* News Service, 02.04.2008.
[37] *Forum 18* News Service, 29.05.2007.
[38] *Forum 18* News Service, 30.05.2007.
[39] *Vatican Radio*, 14.12.2006.
[40] *Forum 18* News Service, 06.06.2007.
[41] *Forum 18* News Service, 28.05.2007.
[42] *Christian Solidarity Worldwide*, CSW Briefing, 30.05.2007; CSW Briefing, 15.06.2007.
[43] *Forum 18* News Service, 05.06.2007.
[44] *Forum 18* News Service, 17.07.2007.
[45] *Forum 18* News Service, 11.10.2007.
[46] *Forum 18* News Service, 07.12.2007.
[47] *Forum 18* News Service, 07.12.2008.
[48] *Forum 18* News Service, 02.04.2008.
[49] *L'Osservatore Romano*, 28.04.2007.
[50] Pope Benedict XVI, *Angelus address*, 30.09.2007.
[51] *Hansard*, 24.05.2007, col. 760.
[52] *ACN (UK) News*, 15.02.2008.
[53] *Xinhua agency*, 19.12.2007.
[54] *Asia News*.
[55] *People's Daily* and *AsiaNews*, 07.02.2007.
[56] Report by Professors Tong Shijun and Liu Zhongyu (Shanghai Normal University). See Wu Jiao , "Religious believers thrice the estimate", *China Daily*, 07.02.2007.
[57] Private correspondence with *Holy Spirit Study Centre*.
[58] *China Aid Association, Forum 18*.
[59] *China Aid Association*, 17.04.2007.
[60] *Asia News*, 12.10.2007.
[61] *China: The Torch of Faith*, ACN (UK) Report, Spring 2008.
[62] *Asia News*, 12.10.2007.
[63] *Asia News*, 22.11.2007.
[64] *South China Morning Post*, 17.12.2007.
[65] *Asia News*, 31.05.2008.

[66] *Ansa*, 06.08.2006; *Radio Giornale*, 07.08.2006.
[67] *Radio Vatican*, 10.09.07.
[68] *Aciprensa*, 13.07.2007.
[69] *Christian Solidarity Worldwide*, CSW Briefing, 24.04.2007.
[70] *Christian Solidarity Worldwide*, CSW Briefing, 26.06.2007; 03.09.2007.
[71] *Aciprensa*, 11.12.2007.
[72] *ACN (UK) News*, 20.02.2008.
[73] ILO Global Report, *Equality at work: Taking the Challenge* (2007).
[74] *ACN (UK) News*, 24.04.2007.
[75] *Figaro Magazine*, 02.06.2007, *France Catholique*, 25.01.2008.
[76] *France Catholique*, 25.01.2008.
[77] *Reuters*, 01.06.2008.
[78] *ACN Newsflash*, 12.06.2008.
[79] *Human Rights Without Frontiers*.
[80] *Catholic Herald*, 06.04.2007.
[81] *An Ancient Faith Renewed: Christians in Ethiopia and across the Horn of Africa*, ACN (UK) Report, Spring 2007.
[82] *Compass Direct News*.
[83] *Open Doors*.
[84] *Compass Direct News*; *Open Doors*, 10.09.2007.
[85]*Evangelical Alliance*, 02.07.2008 <http://www.ea.org.au/ReligiousLiberty/PrayerPostings.aspx>.
[86] *Compass Direct News*, 31.01.2007.
[87] *Compass Direct News*, 13.06.2008.
[88] *Compass Direct News*, 25.02.2008.
[89] *Compass Direct News*, 31.03.2007.
[90] *Catholic News Agency*, 20.03.2008.
[91] *Global Council of Indian Christians*: Persecution Update India, 28.05.2008.
[92] *Global Council of Indian Christians*: Persecution Update India, 29.05.2008.
[93] *AsiaNews*, 09.07.2008
[94] *AsiaNews*, 12.09.2007.
[95] *Compass Direct News*, 02.04.2008.
[96] *Compass Direct News*, 10.03.2008.

[97] *Compass Direct News*, 05.06.2008.
[98] *AsiaNews*, 05.01.2007; *Compass Direct News*, 04.01.2007.
[99] *Compass Direct News*, 08.02.2008; 05.02.2008 statement by the Institute on Religion and Public Policy.
[100] *ACN (UK), News*, 07. 09.2006.
[101] *ACN (UK), News*, 05.06.2008.
[102] *ACN (UK), News*, 22.01.2007.
[103] *ACN (UK), News*, 23.05.2007.
[104] *Reconquête*, Paris, No. 238, 05.2007.
[105] *Zenit*, 08.06.2007.
[106] *ACN (UK), News*, 06.06.2007.
[107] *ACN (UK), News*, 20.06.2007.
[108] *ACN (UK), News*, 27.07.2007.
[109] *ACN (UK), News*, 09.01.2008.
[110] *Scottish Catholic Observer*, 18.01.2008.
[111] *ACN (UK), News*, 18.02.2008.
[112] *ACN (UK), News*, 02 - 04.2008.
[113] *AsiaNews*, 05.04.2008, 07.04.2008.
[114] *AsiaNews*.
[115] Felix Corley, Obituary for Fr Ragheed, *Independent*, 14.06.2007.
[116] Sandro Magister, *The Last Mass of Ragheed, Martyr of the Chaldean Church* <www.chiesa.espresso.repubblica.it >.
[117] Ibid.
[118] Professor Adnam Mokrani, Rome. Cited on *Zenit*, 04.06.2007.
[119] *BBC News*, 21.12.2006.
[120] "Palestine, radiographie d'un développement", *Oasis*, no. 5, 05.2007
[121] *Le Figaro*, 22.06.2007; *La Croix*, 26.06.2007.
[122] *La Croix*, 26.06.2007.
[123] *Le Figaro*, 8.10.2007; *La Croix*, 9.10.2007.
[124] *Petites annonces chrétiennes*, 15.10.2007.
[125] *Catholic Herald*, 21.12.2007.
[126] *Compass Direct News*, 04.06.2008 – Palestinian Centre for Human Rights.
[127] *Forum 18* News Service, 10.05.2008.
[128] *ACN (UK), News*, 11.05.2008.
[129] *Voice of Freedom*, 03.01.2008.
[130] *Forum 18* News Service, 28.09.2007.
[131] *Forum 18* News Service, 25.02.2008.
[132] *Forum 18* News Service, 28.03.2008.
[133] *AsiaNews*, 28.01.2006.
[134] *Forum 18*.
[135] *Forum 18* News Service, 30.01.2008.
[136] *Forum 18* News Service, 15.02.2008.
[137] *Forum 18* News Service, 28.03.2008.
[138] *ACN (UK), News*, 11.06.2008.
[139] *as-Safir*, 06.07.2007.
[140] Ministerial Decree No. 377, 09.06.2007. See ibid.
[141] Officially, the country states it is 100 percent Muslim, so it is impossible to accurately calculate the number of Christians.
[142] *Religious Tolerence*, <http://www.religioustolerance.org/rt_maldive.htm>.
[143] *Project Open Book*, <http://www.domini.org/openbook/malback.htm>.
[144] *Open Doors*, <http://www.opendoors.org.au/index.cfm?page=5>.
[145] *Minivan News*, <http://www.minivannews.com/news/news.php?id=4484>.
[146] *Website of The President's Office, Republic of the Maldives*, <http://www.presidencymaldives.gov.mv/publications/Maldives_Towards_a_New_Dawn.pdf>.
[147] *Compact Direct News*, 10.07.2006; 28.03.2007.
[148] *Compass Direct News*, 16.02.2006.
[149] *Christian Solidarity Worldwide*, CSW Briefing, 20.09.2007.

[150] *Compass Direct News*, 07.03.2007.
[151] *Christian Solidarity Worldwide*, CSW Briefing, 26.06.2007; *Compass Direct News*, 27.03.2007; *HRWF International*, 07.04.2007; *Compass Direct News*, 29.03.2007; *HRWF International*, 30.03.2007; and *ICN News*, 06.06.2007.
[152] *Compact Direct News*, 17.04.2007.
[153] *Compact Direct News*, 29.06.2007.
[154] *Christian Solidarity Worldwide*, CSW Briefing, 01.10.2007; *Compass Direct News*, 05.10.2007; *HRWF International*, 11.10.2007.
[155] *Compact Direct News*, 22.10.2007.
[156] *Compact Direct News*, 26.12.2007.
[157] *Compact Direct News*, 30.10.2007.
[158] *Compact Direct News*, 28.11.2007
[159] *Compact Direct News*, 13.12.2007.
[160] *Compact Direct News*, 13.02.2008.
[161] *Compact Direct News*, 12.02.2008.
[162] Personal correspondence. Information gathered by Rev. Fr. Paulinus Nweke, Coordinator of Interreligious Dialogue, Catholic Archdiocese of Jos through personal discussions and telephone conversations on 20.02.2008.
[163] *Compass Direct News*, 05.03.2008.
[164] *Annuario Pontificio* (2008), pp. 604-05.
[165] *Asia News*, 09.13.2007.
[166] *Asia News*, 04.16.2008; *Compass Direct News*, 25.04.2008.
[167] *ACN (UK) News*, 22.05.2007.
[168] *The News* (India), 30.10.2007.
[169] *Washington Post*, 31.10.2007.
[170] *Minorities' Concern of Pakistan newsletter*, no. 22, 01.2008, p. 1.
[171] Ibid.
[172] *Minorities' Concern of Pakistan newsletter*, no. 23, 02.2008, p. 1.
[173] *ACN (UK) News*, 25.05.2008.

[174] John Thavis, "Pakistani bishops encouraged by Pope to be brave", *Catholic Herald*, 27.06.2008.
[175] NCJP, Pakistan, *The Tablet*, 19.07.08
[176] *ACN (UK) News*, 01.07.2008.
[177] ACN interview April 2008
[178] *Asia News*, 30.01.2006.
[179] *Nezavisimaja gazeta*, 18.09.2006.
[180] *Vedomosti*, 26.09.2006.
[181] *Izvestija*, 18.09.2007, 19.09.2007.
[182] *Forum 18*, 25.09.2007.
[183] *Izvestija*, 14.11.2007.
[184] *La Nuova Europa*, no. 5 (2007), pp. 85-88.
[185] *Interfax*; published by *Forum 18*, 23.10.2007.
[186] *Zenit*, 30.04.2008.
[187] *Forum 18* News Service, 21.01.2008.
[188] *Forum 18* News Service, 28.02.2008.
[189] *Forum 18* News Service, 26.03.2008.
[190] *ACN (UK) News*, 21.04.2008.
[191] US Department of State, *2004 International Religious Freedom Report*.
[192] "Saudi Church Project Runs into the Sand", *Spiegel*, 16.04.2008.
[193] *Compact Direct News*, 20.02.2007.
[194] *UCA News*, 17.12.07
[195] *Compact Direct News*, 21.02.2008.
[196] *Zenit*, 21.04.2008; *The Hindu* 21.04.2008; *Reuters*, 20.04.2008.
[197] *UCA News*, 01.05.2008.
[198] US Department of State, *2007 Report on International Religious Freedom*.
[199] *ACN (UK) News*, 25.01.2007.
[200] *Compass Direct News*, 10.01.2007.
[201] *Compass Direct News*, 03.10.2007.
[202] *Catholic Herald*, 04.05.2007.
[203] *Reuters*, 27.11.2007, *The Guardian*, 04.12.2007.
[204] *Assist News Service*, 05.06.2008.

[205] John Pontifex, Interview (February 2007), *An Ancient Faith Renewed*, ACN (UK) Report, Spring 2007.

[206] European Union, *Turkey Progress Report 2004*.

[207] *La Croix*, 29.01.2007.

[208] *La Croix*, 20.04.2007, 23.11.2007; *Le Monde*, 20.04.2007, 24.11.2007; *Le Figaro*, 20.04.2007; *Compact Direct News*, 19.04.2008.

[209] *Compact Direct News*, 19.07.2007.

[210] *Compact Direct News*, 04.09.2007.

[211] *Compact Direct News*, 05.10.2007.

[212] *La Croix*, 18.12.2007; *Le Monde*, 18.12.2007; *Compact Direct News*, 17.12.2007.

[213] *Compact Direct News*, 08.01.2008.

[214] *AsiaNews* 22.08.2006.

[215] *Forum 18* News Service, 05.09.2007.

[216] *Forum 18* News Service, 19.12.2006.

[217] *Narodnoe Slovo*, 24.04.2007.

[218] *Forum 18* News Service, 20.04.2007.

[219] *Forum 18* News Service, 04.07.2007, 17.09.2007.

[220] *Forum 18* News Service, 17.09.2007.

[221] *Forum 18* News Service, 18.01.2008.

[222] *Forum 18* News Service, 12.03.2008.

[223] *Forum 18* News Service, 29.05.2008.

[224] *Forum 18* News Service, 11.07.2008

[225] Kirk A. Hawkins and David R. Hansen, "Dependent Civil Society: The *Circulos Bolivarianos* in Venezuela" in *The Wall Street Journal* (Eastern edition), 16.06.2006, p. A1.

[226] *Fides*, 17.01.2006.

[227] *Radio Giornale*; *Radio Vatican*, 20.01.2006.

[228] *Zenit*, 21.12.2006.

[229] *Radio Vatican*, 09.01.2007.

[230] *Zenit*, 10.01.2007; *L´Osservatore Romano*, 06.01.2007.

[231] *Fides*, 10.07.2007.

[232] *Radio Vatican*, 19.09.2007.

[233] *Aciprensa*, 02.08.2007.

[234] *Aciprensa*, 08.09.2007; *Aciprensa*, 07.02.2007.

[235] *Fides*, 22.10.2007; *Aciprensa*, 28.11.2007; *La Civilta Cattolica*, 03.03.2007.

[236] *Avvenire*, 14.07.2007; *Aciprensa*, 17.07.2007; *Aciprensa*, 07.08.2007.

[237] *Aciprensa*, 24.07.2008.

[238] *ACN Newsflash*, 19.11.2007.

[239] *Aciprensa*, 06.12.2007.

[240] *Aciprensa*, 09.12.2007.

[241] ACN interview (Italy office)

[242] *Compact Direct News*, 02.11.2007.

[243] David Alton, column in *The Universe*, 06.05.2007.

[244] *Compact Direct News*, 13.08.2007.

[245] *Montagnard Foundation*, 04.02.2008.

[246] *AsiaNews*, 01.02.2008, 04.02.2008.

[247] *Compass Direct News*, 11.03.2008.

[248] *Compass Direct News*, 21.04.2008.

[249] *Montagnard Foundation*, 26.05.2008.

[250] *Pastoral Letter by the Zimbabwe Catholic Bishops' Conference on the Current Crisis of Our Country*, 30.03.2007.

[251] *ACN (UK) News*, 19.02.2008.

[252] *Catholic News*, 23.04.2008.

[253] *ACN (UK) News*, 28.04.2008.

[254] Kitsepile Nyathi, "Zimbabwe: Questions Over Mugabe's Two Million Percent Rise in Support", *The Nation* (Nairobi), 01.07.2008.

[255] *Tear Fund*, Press release 27.01.2007; Zimbabwe Human Rights NGO Forum, *Political Violence Report for January 2007*, 16.03.2007.

[256] *ACN (UK) News*, 23.05.2008.

[257] *Ecumenical News International*, 28.05.2008.

[258] *New York Times*, 16.05.2008; *AFP*, 29.05.2008.

About *Aid to the Church in Need*

Aid to the Church in Need supports Christians wherever they are persecuted, oppressed or in pastoral need. ACN is a Catholic charity, helping to bring Christ to the world.

Founded on Christmas Day 1947 ACN is now a universal pastoral charity of the Catholic Church, with thousands of projects all over the world. In 2007 the charity responded to 5,096 requests for aid from bishops and religious superiors in 136 countries:

- Seminarians are trained

- Bibles and religious literature are printed

- Priests and religious are supported

- Refugees are helped

- Churches and chapels are built and restored

- Over 45 million of ACN's Child's Bible have been printed in more than 150 languages

- Religious programmes are broadcast

For regular updates from the suffering Church around the world and to view our full range of books, cards, gifts and music, please log on to ACN's national website in your country (see over).

> *Thank you for helping to dry the tears of the abandoned Jesus on the crosses of this century.*
>
> Fr Werenfried van Straaten, O. Praem,
> founder of *Aid to the Church in Need*

 **Aid to the Church in Need**

Aid to the Church in Need
United Kingdom

12-14 Benhill Avenue
Sutton
Surrey
SM1 4DA
United Kingdom

Telephone: +44 (0) 20 8642 8668
Email: acn@acnuk.org
Website: www.acnuk.org

Australia

PO Box 6245
Blacktown DC
NSW 2148
Australia

Telephone: +61 (0) 2 9679 1929
Email: info@aidtochurch.org
Website: www.aidtochurch.org

Canada

P.O. Box 670, STN H
Montreal
QC H3G 2M6
Canada

Telephone: +1 514 932 0552
     or +1 800 585 6333
Email: info@acn-aed-ca.org
Website: www.acn-aed-ca.org

Ireland

151 St Mobhi Road
Glasnevin
Dublin 9
Ireland

Telephone: +353 (0) 1 83 77 516
Email: churchinneed@eircom.net
Website: www.acnirl.org

United States of America

725 Leonard Street
PO Box 220384
Brooklyn NY 11222-0384
USA

Telephone: +1 (1) 800 628 6333
Email: info@churchinneed.org
Website: www.churchinneed.org

International Headquarters

ACN International
(Postal Address)

Bischof-Kindermann-Straße 23
D-61462 Königstein/Ts.
Germany

Telephone: +49 (0) 61 74 291 0
Email: kinoph@acn-intl.org
Website: www.acn-intl.org

ACN International
(P.O. Box Address)

Postfach 12 09
D-61452 Königstein/Ts.
Germany